Goose-Pimple

A Play

Devised by
Mike Leigh

Samuel French — London
New York – Sydney – Toronto – Hollywood

GOOSE-PIMPLES

Devised by Mike Leigh

First performed at the Hampstead Theatre, London, on 3 March 1981, when the cast was as follows:

Vernon	Jim Broadbent
Jackie	Marion Bailey
Irving	Paul Jesson
Frankie	Jill Baker
Muhammad	Antony Sher

Devised and directed by Mike Leigh
Designed by Caroline Beaver

The same production opened at the Garrick Theatre, London, on 29 April 1981

Goose-Pimples was evolved from scratch entirely by rehearsal through improvisation

The action takes place in Vernon's flat

ACT I	Scene 1	Late Spring. Early morning
	Scene 2	Two days later. Early evening
	Scene 3	Later the same evening
ACT II		A few minutes later

Time—the present

NOTE

The Arabic in this text has not been expressed phonetically. We have kept to the standard spelling, as used by the Linguaphone Institute.

It is therefore essential for actors playing Muhammad to consult Arabic speakers for the Arabic pronunciation itself, and, if possible, Saudi Nationals for the pronunciation of the English.

The following are the names of towns and villages in Saudi Arabia referred to by Muhammad: Abha, Arafat, Dhahran, Jiddha (Jeddah), Mecca, Mina, Muzdalifah, Taif.

ACT I

Scene 1

Vernon's flat. An early morning in late spring

The flat is on the second floor of a block of flats purpose-built around 1935. The lounge and dining areas are in a double room, which was designed originally as two rooms with folding doors between them, but the doors have been removed. In the lounge area are a black leather sofa and swivel armchair, a side table, a bar with bar-stools, a music centre with cassettes and records underneath, a television and an imitation leopard-skin rug. In the dining area, there are four chrome dining chairs, a table and a wall-unit, on the shelves of which are a few paperbacks, two or three small school sports trophies and a telephone. The walls are papered with tiger-skin wallpaper (or something similar). There are no pictures, but several mirrors and veteran car motifs. The doors to the two areas are close to each other, and have frosted-glass panes. On the door in the dining area, one of the panes has been replaced at some time by a clear pane. Across the hall is the kitchenette, a small part of which is visible. The front door and the other rooms cannot be seen

When the Curtain *rises, the room is empty*

Vernon enters, wearing a track suit. He is out of breath, and is sweating a little. He picks up an executive case from a bar-stool. He puts it on the dining-table, and opens it. He takes out a diary. He takes the telephone from the wall-unit, and puts it on the table. He flicks through the diary

Jackie enters

Jackie Hi.

Vernon Good morning, Jackie. How are you?

Jackie All right. Been jogging?

Vernon Indeed I have. Still up? (*He dials*)

Jackie Yeh. I don't really feel tired this morning. We had a really busy night, you know—you don't want to go to bed when you get back.

Vernon No?

Jackie Had your shower yet?

Vernon No—just making a quick phone call.

Jackie Oh. I might have a bath. Is that a business call?

Vernon Yeh.

Jackie Oh, really? 'S a bit early.

Vernon It's the only time I can get hold of this geezer.

Jackie I know, it's the best time to get 'em, you know—when they're not expecting it.

Vernon It was his idea I should call at this ungodly hour.

Jackie Oh, really?

Vernon I've got a feeling he wants to cancel his order—got fed up with waiting.

Jackie What was it, another Metro?

Vernon Yes. Started talking about getting a Datsun now, hasn't he.

Jackie 'Ow long's 'e been waiting, then?

Vernon Nine weeks now.

Jackie 'T's bad, init? Makes you look stupid, you know.

Vernon Not bloody kidding it makes me look stupid—always ends up on our bloody doorstep, I tell you.

Jackie That's right. It's a nice little car, though, a Metro. 'T's perky, you know?

Vernon Try again. (*He dials again*)

Jackie It's not really a status car, though, is it?

Vernon So you're working Saturday night, are you?

Jackie That's right—well I'm on early shift, you know?

Pause

Is your girl-friend coming over, as well?

Vernon No—just a threesome.

Jackie Oh, really?

Vernon She's going down to Swindon for the weekend.

Jackie What's she going down there for?

Vernon She's taking her kiddy down to see his dad.

Jackie Oh, really? That's a bit of a drag for her, init?

Vernon Suppose so. It's not my problem.

Jackie No, that's right. It don't pay to get too involved, you know.

Vernon (*into the receiver*) Come on!

Jackie Who's doing the cooking, then?

Vernon Yours truly.

Jackie Oh, really?

Vernon I'm quite a good chef, Jackie.

Jackie Oh. What you 'avin?

Vernon Steak.

Jackie Oh, yeh . . . well, you can't go wrong with steak, y'know?

Vernon What time d'you finish Saturday night?

Jackie Ten.

Vernon You're very welcome to join us for a drink if you get back in time.

Jackie Oh, thanks, yeh—well, I don't really know yet, you know, I might be going on somewhere with some friends after work, probably go to a club or something, go out for a meal.

Vernon Feel free.

Jackie Mm. Your friends goin'a be stayin' late?

Vernon I should imagine so, knowing these two.

Jackie Oh, really?

Vernon More than likely outstay their welcome.

Jackie Oh, well, you just got to tell people.

*Vernon slams down the receiver and paces round the room, thrusting at the
air with a squash-racket he has picked up*

Vernon Oh, for Christ's sake, what's the bloody point! Tells me to phone,
then he's not sodding there!

Jackie It's bad business. I mean you're doin' 'im a favour.

Vernon I don't exactly enjoy starting work an hour and a half early, I can
tell you.

Jackie No, 't's right.

*Vernon puts the telephone away, puts the diary back in the case, and puts the
case on the floor in the corner*

D'you play squash last night?

Vernon Yes.

Jackie D'you lose again?

Vernon No, I won, as it happens.

Jackie Oh, did you? What did your friend say?

Vernon He paid up, didn't he?

Jackie 'T's right. 'E's got to, 'asn't 'e? If that's the agreement. You know,
it's like business.

Vernon You're right, Jackie. You don't know how right you are.

Vernon exits to his room, taking his squash-racket with him

Jackie These blokes, they say they're goin' to do something, and when it
comes to the crunch, they back out. Thing is, Vern, if you think some-
one's going to pull a stroke like that, you've got to tell 'em where you
stand, straight off. They may not like it, but the end justifies the means.

Vernon (*off*) That's right.

Jackie Yeh, you've just got to be straight with people. Especially if there's
a lot of big money changing hands. It's only good sense in the long run.
You get these cowboys, but let's face it, anyone with a bit of savvy's not
going to get stung twice, are they?

Vernon (*off*) No.

Jackie I mean, once you've 'ad a bit of experience in selling, you can
recognize a duff customer; you've just got to be straight with 'em, you
know, say, "Look, don't waste my time, and I won't waste yours,
right?" Yeh, you've really got to believe in your product, you know,
when you're selling, got to be a bit pushy, yeh? I don't mean pressurize
people, but you've got to be positive. It's no use askin' if they want to
buy, you've got to tell 'em they do want to buy, I mean, you're doin'
them a favour, really. Yeh, it's all about SATOC, you know.

Vernon (*off*) You what?

Jackie SATOC, yeh? You gotta Show the Advantage of your product,
Turn the customer's Objections, and Close the sale. SATOC, yeh?
S-A-T-O-C.

Vernon (*off*) Oh, by the way, Jackie—when can you let me have the rent?

Jackie When d'you wannit?

Vernon (*off*) It was due last Sunday.

Jackie Yes, well I haven't really seen you, you know?
Vernon (*off*) Write us out a cheque, leave it on the table.
Jackie Yeh, all right!

Jackie goes into the hall quickly. She exits into her own room, and slams the door

The Lights quickly fade to a Black-out

SCENE 2

The same. Two days later. Early evening

Vernon enters, dressed informally, with a tray of nuts. He makes several trips to the kitchen for the rest of the food

He puts on a Rod Stewart record, then goes to the wall-unit and takes out cutlery, glasses, etc. He sets the table for three, quickly and efficiently, putting a plate of melon and a dinner roll at each place. Then he pours himself a whisky and settles down with it at the bar. The doorbell rings immediately. Vernon lowers the volume of the music, and then goes into the hall

He exits to answer the front door

Vernon (*off*) Hello!
Irving (*off*) Hello, Vernon.

Irving enters with a bottle of red wine (wrapped)

Vernon (*off*) Hello, Frankie—very glad you could make it.
Frankie (*off*) Are you?

The front door closes

Irving Got a bottle of wine for you, Vernon—here you are.

Frankie and Vernon enter

Frankie Oh, what a super flat!
Vernon (*unwrapping the bottle*) Oh, you shouldn't have bothered!
Irving Oh, I see, you've got a choice of doors, then, have you, eh?
Vernon Yes, this room has a divide facility, an option I chose not to take up.
Irving Oh, really?
Vernon I just whipped the dividing doors out.
Frankie Well, it gives the illusion of it being bigger than it is, doesn't it, Ver?
Vernon Frankie—let me take your coat.
Frankie Thank you.
Irving (*looking at the walls*) I've never seen anything like this before, Vernon.
Vernon The wallpaper? Yes, I'm quite pleased with it.
Irving Did you shoot it yourself, eh?

Vernon and Irving laugh uproariously

Vernon exits with Frankie's coat

Frankie (*inspecting the table*) Oh, this looks nice, doesn't it?
Irving So this is the famous bar, then, is it, eh?

Vernon enters

Vernon Yes—it's a little bit special isn't it?
Irving It certainly is.
Vernon And you've got to admit it's me.
Irving All you need now is the barmaid to go with it, eh?
Vernon No shortage of barmaids here, Irving, I can assure you of that!
Irving I'm sure there's not, no!

Vernon and Irving laugh uproariously

Frankie Of course, we wouldn't be happy with a small flat, would we, darling?
Vernon As a matter of fact, Frankie, it's a very spacious flat, and I personally don't feel cramped in any way.
Frankie No.
Vernon And it certainly fulfils my every requirement to the letter.
Irving And we all know about your requirements, don't we, eh?

Vernon and Irving laugh uproariously

Vernon Frankie—would you like to sit down, make yourself comfortable?
Frankie Thank you. (*She sits down on the sofa*)
Irving I hope the wine fits in with the menu, Vernon.
Vernon Oh, I'm sure it will, Irving.
Irving Should be warm enough—I was holding it between my thighs in the car. (*He laughs uproariously*)

Frankie takes out a cigarette

Vernon Frankie—let me give you a light. There you are. (*He lights her cigarette*)
Frankie Thank you.
Vernon Get you an ashtray. (*He places one next to her*)
Frankie Thank you.
Vernon Frankie: what can I get you to drink?
Frankie Bacardi and Coke, please, Ver.
Vernon Bacardi I do not have.
Irving Oh, caught him out, have you?
Frankie Oh, it doesn't matter—I'll have a gin and tonic.
Vernon Gin and tonic. Same for you, Irving, if I'm not very much mistaken?
Irving As per usual—you know my tastes, eh?
Vernon Indeed I do.

Vernon and Irving laugh uproariously. Pause. Frankie utters a subconscious, but quite loud, monosyllabic "Oh!"; this means, vaguely, a combination of

"Well, here we all are!" and *"Oh dear, isn't life painful?"* Hereafter,
"Frankie utters" refers to this ejaculation

Irving Well, this is cosy.

Vernon (*pouring the drinks*) So, you managed to find the old place all right, then?

Frankie No problem at all, Ver.

Irving I thought it was wise to give the North Circular a miss.

Frankie I was driving.

Vernon Were you, Frankie?

Frankie I was.

Irving Yes, we had to come in Frankie's car.

Vernon Oh, what's wrong with the Metro this time?

Irving Couldn't get it started.

Vernon Done it again, have you, Irving?

Irving No, carburettor's on the blink—I shall have to swap it next week.

Vernon What are you going to swap it for?

Irving Dunno . . . That Applejack HLE.

Frankie Oh, no—not Applejack!

Irving What?

Vernon Too late—I've sold it.

Irving When?

Vernon First thing this morning.

Irving You move fast—who to?

Vernon Our friend Mr Tench.

Irving I thought he'd decided he was getting a Datsun.

Vernon So did he till I changed his mind for him. Ice, Frankie?

Frankie Please.

Irving Well, you've got him off your back at last, anyway.

Vernon You're not bloody kidding, Irving. (*He hands out the drinks*)

Irving You've certainly got yourself well set up here, Vernon.

Frankie There's a nasty smell on your stairs, Ver.

Vernon No, no, Frankie, that's just the fluid the cleaners use.

Frankie Oh. Smells a bit like a public lavatory to me.

Vernon Is that a fact, Frankie? I don't frequent public lavatories. (*Offering a tray of nuts*) Can I tempt you?

Irving You don't want to pick anything up, do you?

Vernon and Irving laugh uproariously

Vernon (*sitting down*) No, as a matter of fact, under the terms of the lease, the management are required to keep the common parts of these flats— the stairwells, the halls and forecourts, and the parking area—in an orderly and hygienic condition, and I must say, to their eternal credit, this is adhered to, which I think you'll agree is a blessing in these days of shoddy workmanship and poor service.

Frankie There's not much parking space, though, is there?

Vernon You park at the front, did you?

Frankie Mm.

Vernon Yes, it's sometimes a bit tricky at the front, but there's ample facility at the rear.

Irving Bit like Raquel Welch, eh?

Frankie Why don't you come and sit down, darling?

Irving Ample facility at the rear, eh?

Vernon and Irving laugh uproariously

Vernon Well, I must say, it's nice to see you again, Frankie.

Frankie It's nice to see you, too, Ver.

Vernon And how've you been?

Frankie Absolutely fine, thank you.

Vernon Oh, what've you been up to?

Frankie Well, we've been terribly busy, haven't we, darling?

Irving Oh yes—very active, eh? (*He laughs uproariously*)

Frankie We've been eating out a tremendous amount.

Irving That's right.

Frankie Socializing—you know?

Vernon Oh, yes?

Frankie Seeing a lot of our friends.

Vernon Oh, jolly good.

Irving Who?

Frankie Sit down, sweetheart. And how have you been, Ver?

Vernon Oh, very well indeed, Frankie. These last few weeks I've been rushed off my feet, I can't tell you.

Frankie I'm sure you have.

Irving Who've we been seeing, then?

Frankie Eh?

Irving Who've we been seeing?

Frankie Then of course we're going on our holidays soon, aren't we?

Irving (*sitting next to Frankie on the sofa*) We haven't been seeing anybody.

Frankie Aren't we?

Irving What?

Frankie Going on our holiday in five weeks?

Irving Oh, yeh, Corfu.

Frankie That's right.

Irving Five weeks today, and we'll be there.

Vernon Yes, yes; that sounds very exciting.

Frankie We're looking forward to it, aren't we?

Irving We certainly are—all those beach balls bouncing around, eh? (*He laughs uproariously*)

Vernon Cheers!

Irving⎫
Frankie⎭ (*together*) Cheers!

Vernon And welcome to my humble abode, such as it is. It's very nice to have you both here at long last.

Irving It's very nice to be here, at long last.

Frankie Darling—your hair's sticking up again.

Irving That's not all that's sticking up, eh? (*He laughs uproariously*)

Vernon No, I must say I envy you your holiday plans, but I never go away in the summer. I take a few days off during Wimbledon fortnight, which is something I enjoy, but, unlike Irving, here, I can't justify turning my back on the busiest period of the year, profit-wise.

Irving Oh, no: August is when it really picks up—we'll be back long before then.

Vernon No, no, Irving; the time to sell a motor car is from May to September—that's when people want to buy. It's a well-known fact, Frankie.

Irving Don't listen to him—he doesn't know what he's talking about.

Frankie We can afford our holiday, Ver.

Vernon I'm sure you can, Frankie, and your financial affairs are none of my business. Would you like a nibble? (*He offers the nuts*)

Irving Oh. I'll have a nibble. Eh? (*He laughs uproariously*)

Frankie eats some nuts

Vernon Why don't you just hang on to those, Frankie? No, I take my major break in the winter, which, I think you'll agree, is the time to get away from this God-forsaken climate.

Irving Well, this is it.

Frankie We had a winter holiday once, didn't we, sweetheart?

Vernon Oh, yes—you went ski-ing.

Frankie That's right.

Vernon Yes. Irving's told me about that.

Frankie Oh, has he? What did you tell him?

Irving Well . . . we had a good time. Didn't we?

Frankie Oh yes, it was absolutely super. I love ski-ing.

Vernon and Irving laugh uproariously

Vernon Yes, but it's not the same as getting away to the sun, though, is it?

Frankie Well, you'd be surprised, Ver; you can get a super sun-tan on top of the Alps, you know.

Irving Oh yes: the sun reflects off the snow every bit as much as it does off the sand, you know.

Frankie That's right.

Vernon Ah, yes; but it doesn't compare with lying back on the beach, soaking up the sun, with that wonderful aroma of Ambre Solaire hanging on the breeze.

Frankie No, and that's exactly why we don't go away in the winter any more. We've been going to Ibiza for a few years, haven't we, sweetheart?

Irving Mm.

Frankie But to be absolutely honest with you, Ver, it has got a bit crowded recently.

Irving Yes, we've given up Ibiza as a bad job, you know.

Frankie That's right.

Irving It's become overrun with Germans.

Vernon Oh, no, no, no. I can't be doing with the Germans. The only kind

of German I like is blonde, nubile, preferably on its back, and of the
female variety.

Vernon and Irving laugh uproariously

Irving And how is Astrid, by the way?
Vernon Very well indeed, thank you, Irving.
Irving Good.
Frankie Who's that, then, Ver?
Vernon A young friend of mine.
Frankie Oh yes?
Irving What's she up to tonight, then, eh?
Vernon Looking after the kiddies, I expect.
Frankie Oh, she's got kids, has she?
Irving No—she's an au pair Vernon picked up.
Vernon She's a young German girl, she's working over here, she hasn't
got many friends, so I took it upon myself to—shall we say?—entertain
her.
Irving Show her the sights, eh?

Vernon and Irving laugh uproariously

Frankie How old is she, Ver?
Vernon Why do you ask, Frankie?
Frankie I was just wondering.
Vernon She's eighteen.
Frankie Bit young for you, isn't it?
Vernon It's legal, Frankie. And let's face it, these young girls can teach us
older men a thing or two.
Irving The younger ones refresh the parts the older ones cannot reach, eh?

Vernon and Irving laugh uproariously

Vernon Like it! Like it!
Irving And, talking of which, how's the lodger, by the way?
Vernon She's fine, thank you, Irving.
Irving Fitting in well, is she?
Vernon No problems at all.
Irving And how are you fitting in with her, then, eh?
Vernon I don't see what you're driving at, Irving.
Irving Oh, come on, Vernon!
Vernon No, no, no, you've lost me completely. The arrangement I have
with my lodger is strictly business.
Frankie Oh, really?
Vernon I don't mix business with pleasure, Frankie.
Frankie No.
Vernon It's not advisable, no matter how attractive the prospect may
seem.

Irving picks up the nude statuette

Irving Is this your mascot, then, Vernon, eh?

Vernon Careful, Irving—that's an *objet d'art*, for Christ's sake!
Frankie Put it down, darling, please.
Irving Very nice, isn't it? Eh? I shall have to get one of these—in the flesh. (*He puts the statuette back*)
Vernon I thought you had one.
Irving Yeh. Well . . . not quite this shape, eh? (*He laughs uproariously*)
Frankie There's no need to be rude, Irving.

Pause

She's a croupier, isn't she, your lodger?
Irving ⎱(*together*)⎰ Yes, she is.
Vernon ⎰   ⎱ That's right.
Frankie Now, that wouldn't suit me.
Vernon No?
Frankie No. Because, quite frankly, Ver, I don't altogether approve of gambling.
Vernon Don't you, Frankie?
Frankie No. So I wouldn't want to put myself in a position whereby I was encouraging it in any way.
Irving Oh yeh? And what sort of position is that, then, eh? (*He laughs uproariously*)
Frankie No, and I have to say, Ver, I think it's immoral.
Vernon It's a free country, Frankie, and I think we ought to leave it up to the individual to make up his or her own mind with regard to this one.
Frankie Oh, of course—each to his own.
Irving Yeh, but only as a last resort, eh? (*He laughs uproariously*)
Frankie No, the fact is, though, Ver, I couldn't actually stand all those men oggling at me all the time, either.
Irving Well, they wouldn't be looking at you, anyway. (*Getting up*) Come on, Vernon, let's have a look around the flat, see what you've made of the place.

Irving goes into the hall and exits towards Vernon's bedroom

Vernon (*getting up*) Yes, of course, Irving. Frankie, would you like to have a look around?
Frankie I wouldn't mind.

Vernon leans over Frankie from behind, and puts his hand on her breast

(*Getting up*) I don't know how you can do that, Ver.

Frankie goes into the hall, followed by Vernon

Frankie exits to the kitchen

Vernon exits to his bedroom

Irving (*off*) Good suspension on the bed, Vernon.
Vernon (*off*) Oh, you've found my bedroom, have you, Irving?
Irving (*off*) Yes!
Vernon (*off*) Yes, it's a good bed!

Irving (*off*) Nice big one, eh?
Vernon (*off*) Well—the bigger the better!
Irving (*off*) Yes, that's what I always say!

Vernon and Irving laugh uproariously, off

Frankie (*off*) Your kitchen's a bit cramped, Vernon.

Irving crosses the hall and goes towards Jackie's room

Irving (*off*) Is this the lodger's room, then, Vernon?

Vernon appears in the hall

Vernon I don't think you need to go in there, Irving.

Frankie comes out of the kitchen and starts to follow Irving

Frankie Oh, I'm sure she wouldn't mind, being as you've got such a good business relationship.
Vernon No, the point is, Frankie, the agreement I have with my lodger is that we respect each other's privacy—it's as simple as that.
Frankie Well, I only want a little peep.

Frankie exits towards Jackie's room

Vernon Frankie, please!
Frankie (*off*) Oh Christ! She isn't very tidy, is she?
Vernon (*moving into the lounge*) Whether she's tidy or not is of no concern to me. What Jackie does in her own room is her business. As long as she's tidy around the rest of the flat, that's all I ask.

Frankie enters

Frankie (*as she enters*) Now, don't get me wrong, Ver—I didn't mean to intrude.
Vernon I'm sorry, Frankie. And I certainly didn't mean to infer that you were a snoop.
Frankie So, what have you been up to, eh?
Vernon Oh, you know. This and that.
Frankie No, I don't know. That's why I'm asking.
Vernon I don't know what you're talking about.
Frankie Been having a good social life, have you?
Vernon Oh, I can't complain. Shall we eat? Would you like to sit here, Frankie?
Frankie Thank you. (*She sits at the table*) I must say I am feeling rather hungry.
Vernon You're looking rather tasty.

Vernon exits to the kitchen

Frankie butters her roll busily and proceeds to eat it avidly

Vernon enters with an opened bottle of white wine

Oh, yes. I see what you mean. You are a hungry girl.

Frankie Why didn't you phone me?
Vernon I'm sorry, Frankie?
Frankie You never phoned me up.
Vernon Oh that! Oh, you want to talk about it now, do you? This is an ideal moment, isn't it? Why don't we just wait for Irving? Where is Irving, by the way? Is he going to join us later? Is that the plan?

Frankie gets up and goes to the door

Frankie Irving!
Irving (*off*) What? Oh, yes—just coming!
Frankie What are you up to?

Irving enters

Irving Nothing. What's the matter?
Frankie (*caressing his hair*) Nothing, darling. Sit down.
Irving Don't do that!
Vernon Irving, would you like to sit here?
Irving Oh, right, thank you. (*He sits down*)
Frankie (*sitting*) D'you mind if I start, Ver?
Vernon (*sitting*) No, by all means, Frankie, tuck in! (*He pours the wine*)
Irving This looks nice.
Frankie Got any ginger, Ver?
Vernon Ginger? No.
Irving Oh, you have to have ginger on melon, you know.
Frankie Oh, yes: it complements the flavour.
Vernon Is that a fact? Well, that's very interesting. I didn't know that.
Frankie Well, you'll remember next time.
Vernon Yes. Ginger and melon. Well, I've learned something new this evening, haven't I? That's an added bonus, isn't it?
Irving Is she a tall girl, Vernon?
Vernon Is who a tall girl, Irving?
Irving Jackie.
Vernon No, she's not, as it happens.
Irving She's as tall as you, though, isn't she?
Vernon Irving, I'm six-foot-two. If Jackie was six-foot-two, I would say, without any doubt, she was a tall girl.
Irving Yeh, well, I've seen some tall girls in my time, eh? (*He laughs uproariously*)
Vernon I'm sure you have. As a matter of fact, Jackie's quite petite.
Irving Oh. I could have sworn she'd be tall.
Vernon You like tall girls, do you Irving?
Frankie I'm five-foot-seven, Ver.
Vernon Yes, of course, you're a tall girl, aren't you, Frankie?
Frankie I'm five-foot-seven, Ir, but I'm not six-foot-two, and if I was six-foot-two, I wouldn't just be tall, I'd be huge. Stupid bugger.
Vernon Mind you, you are quite a big girl, aren't you, Frankie?
Frankie And what exactly do you mean by that, Vernon?
Vernon Would you like some sugar on your melon?

Frankie No, thank you. We have it quite a lot, don't we, darling?
Irving Yeh, we do, don't we, eh!

Vernon and Irving laugh uproariously

Frankie Melon!
Irving Yeh—I know!
Frankie I like to ring the changes.
Vernon I imagine you have ginger on it, though, don't you?
Irving Yeh, we do—sprinkled all over it! (*He laughs uproariously*)
Frankie It's a nice ripe one, this, isn't it?
Irving Yeh. Here, Vernon: do you know how to buy a melon in the greengrocer's? You have to give it a squeeze to see if it's ripe; you push the end in with your finger, and if it gives just a little bit, you know it's ready!

Vernon and Irving laugh uproariously

Frankie Oh, please! (*She finishes her melon*)

Pause. Frankie utters her noise, q.v.

Vernon My word, that slipped down very easily, didn't it, Frankie?
Irving Not half as easily as it slips up! (*He laughs uproariously*)
Frankie Have you got any more, Ver?
Vernon Yes, of course, Frankie—I'm sorry, I should've remembered: the ever-open door! Irving, would you like some more?
Irving Oh, yes please—thank you.

Vernon takes their plates and exits to the kitchen

Frankie Can I give you a hand?

Frankie exits to the kitchen

(*Inaudibly, off*) Why didn't you phone me?

Vernon enters, with more melon, followed by Frankie

I asked you a question.
Vernon I'm sorry, Frankie, what question was that? I was miles away—I must have been thinking about something else. Here you are, Irving.
Irving Oh, thank you.
Vernon Frankie just asked me a question.
Irving Oh?
Vernon Come on, Frankie, sit down. You've got a lot to get through. More wine, Irving?
Irving Yes, please.
Vernon (*pouring the wine*) It's not a bad wine, is it?
Irving No.
Vernon As a light, fruity wine, I find it most acceptable. It's certainly one of my standbys.
Frankie It's a bit dry.

Vernon It is a little bit dry, yes, but I like a dry wine. Perhaps that's just one of the hazards of having a sophisticated palate. Who knows?

Irving She is a redhead, though, isn't she?

Vernon Is who a redhead, Irving?

Irving Jackie.

Vernon No, Jackie is not a redhead, and she's not six-foot-two. She's a petite brunette. Compris? Now, if you'll excuse me, I'll go and get on with the main course.

Vernon exits to the kitchen

Frankie What's the matter with you?

Irving Eh?

Frankie Oh, for Christ's sake. (*She crosses to her bag and takes out a cigarette*)

Irving Having an inter-course cigarette, then, are you, eh? (*He laughs uproariously*)

Frankie Yes, that's right, Irving.

Irving continues to snigger. Pause. Frankie inspects the room

It's all a bit stark, isn't it?

Irving What?

Frankie It's not my cup of tea.

Irving Yeh, well—it's masculine.

Frankie Mm . . . could do with a woman's touch, couldn't it?

Irving Yeh, well, there's no shortage of that around here, is there, eh? Hey, Vernon!

Vernon enters, wearing a naughty apron

Vernon What's that, Irving?

Irving I say—there's no shortage of the woman's touch around here, is there, eh? (*He laughs uproariously*)

Frankie exits to the kitchen

Vernon No, no; no shortage of that.

Irving Oh, I like your pinny.

Vernon Oh, yes. Yes. Well, it does the job.

Irving Keeps the splashes off, eh?

Vernon picks up the wine Irving has brought

Vernon Oh, yes . . . yes, I've seen this one in the supermarket.

Irving It's supposed to be quite good.

Vernon Mm . . . it's always worth taking a risk, isn't it?

Frankie (*off*) Oh, Christ!

Vernon What's wrong now, Frankie?

Frankie enters

Frankie Have you smelt your steak, Ver?

Vernon No, Frankie, I haven't smelt my steak. I was under the impression it was still in the packet.

Frankie Well, just go and give it a sniff.
Vernon What's wrong with it?
Frankie Just go and smell it.
Vernon All right.

Vernon exits to the kitchen, followed by Irving

Frankie Jesus Christ! (*She sits on the sofa and eats some nuts*)

Irving enters, much amused

Irving Ooh, what a pong—eh?

He goes back to the kitchen

(*Off*) Aw! It's really horrible, isn't it?

Irving enters with one of the steaks in its packet

Look at it!
Frankie Oh, take it away, for Christ's sake!
Irving Where d'you get it?

Vernon enters

Vernon In the supermarket.
Frankie Fatal. *Never* buy steak in the supermarket, Ver. You should know that.
Vernon Where d'you expect me to buy it?
Frankie At the butcher's.

Vernon exits to the kitchen

Irving Look!
Frankie I don't want to look at it. Dear, oh dear. I suppose they're all the same, are they?

Vernon enters with the other two steaks in their packets

Vernon Course they're all the same—I got them in the same bloody shop. Jesus Christ, I don't believe this, I don't bloody believe it.
Frankie Well, you'll have to take them back.
Vernon I'm going to report these bastards to the Area Health Authority, I'll take them to court! One mouthful of this garbage we could've all gone down with food-poisoning, could've bloody killed us. I'll sue these sods for every penny they've got, I'll get them closed down if it's the last thing I do. (*As he speaks, he takes a pocket calculator from his case*) It's not as if you don't have to pay for it—it costs a bloody fortune—look at this: two pounds four pence; two pounds seven pence . . .
Irving One ninety-eight.
Vernon God Almighty! Six pounds nine pence! You spend six pounds nine pence on best steak and what d'you wind up with? Putrified bloody horsemeat!
Frankie Well, there's no point in getting in a state about it, Ver.

During the following, Vernon goes and puts the steaks in the kitchen, and returns

He sits at the table, gulping down some wine and a bit of his bread roll

Vernon I'm going to take this in, Monday morning, and ram it down that bastard's throat. He won't know what's bloody hit him. I'll stuff it up his backside. I've had trouble with that sod before; sold me some rancid butter, didn't he?

Irving What, and you went back there?

Vernon Course I went back there, Irving, there's nowhere else to go—all the other shops have closed down, you're left with bloody supermarkets!

Irving Oh, well, you've got to watch everything you buy these days.

Frankie Yes, it's true—look at our wall-unit.

Irving Yeh—unbelievable.

Frankie Disgusting.

Irving Had a great gouge out of the end!

Frankie That's right—I said we should've gone to Brent Cross.

Irving That wouldn't have made any difference.

Frankie And the hair-drier—look what happened to that.

Irving Nearly blew her ear off.

Frankie Took it back to the shop, and they said, "Where's the guarantee?"

Irving Turned into black melted plastic.

Frankie And the washing-machine: that flooded the kitchen after a week, didn't it?

Irving I came home, and she was paddling!

Frankie You don't need a guarantee, do you?

Irving No, not if you know your Consumers' Rights: I told them, it's the retailer's responsibility to ensure that goods are of merchantable quality.

Frankie That's right!

Vernon I'll give this bloody retailer "merchantable quality"! Right: get your coats on. We're going out.

Vernon puts his apron over the back of one of the dining-chairs, and exits to his bedroom

Irving Where are we going?

Vernon (*off*) I'm taking you out for a meal.

Irving Oh, that's good, isn't it?

Frankie picks up the apron, and exits to the kitchen

Irving What are you doing?

Frankie (*off*) Nothing!

Irving Eh?

Vernon enters, wearing a bomber jacket

Vernon Are you ready?

Irving Oh, yes. Ready and willing. Where are you taking us?

Vernon Schooner. (*He switches off the music centre*)

Irving Oh, great. Which one?
Vernon Wembley. (*He switches off the lamp on the bar*)
Irving Hendon one's good.
Vernon We're going to Wembley. (*He switches off the lamp on the wall-unit*)
Irving Hendon's nearer, though.
Vernon We're going to Wembley, Irving.

Frankie enters, wearing Vernon's apron, and with a kitchen knife in one hand and an unpeeled raw onion in the other

Frankie Have you got any mixed herbs, Ver?
Vernon Christ almighty, Frankie—what are you playing at?
Irving What are you doing?
Frankie I'm just going to whip something up—it won't take me five minutes.
Irving Vernon's taking us out for a meal.
Frankie Well, there's no need, is there? Sit down, relax, enjoy yourselves. I'll be back in a moment.

Frankie exits to the kitchen

Irving and Vernon follow her into the hall

Vernon There's nothing in the kitchen, Frankie!
Frankie (*off*) I'm going to make a vegetable gratin.
Vernon (*returning to the lounge*) I don't want vegetables, *I want meat*! God almighty!

Frankie returns. She takes off the apron, and replaces it on the chair

Frankie All right, please yourself. I was only trying to help.

Vernon exits to get Frankie's coat

Irving What's the matter with you? It's a free meal!
Frankie Irving!
Irving Shall we follow in our car?

Vernon enters with Frankie's coat

Vernon We'll take my car.
Irving Oh, right. That'll save petrol.

Irving finishes his glass of wine, whilst Vernon helps Frankie on with her coat, touching her body momentarily as he does so. This is not seen by Irving

Vernon Right. I'm sorry about all this. It's a total disaster, and I'm deeply, deeply ashamed.
Frankie Well, there's no need to apologize, Ver.
Vernon There's every need to apologize, Frankie.
Frankie Well, come along, let's go if we're going; I'm starving.

During the following, Frankie and Irving move into the hall. Vernon switches off the main light and follows them. He switches off the kitchen light

Irving Which way are we going?
Vernon Underpass.
Irving Neasden?
Vernon Of course bloody Neasden!
Irving No, no, no—you want to cut through to the Harrow Road.
Vernon Don't be stupid, Irving.

They exit L

Irving (*off*) That brings you right out into Wembley Central.

The front door is heard opening

Vernon (*off*) I know the way, Irving.

The hall light goes out

Irving (*off*) You want the Broadway, don't you?
Vernon (*off*) I'll do it my way, Irving.

The front door closes, and the Lights fade fairly quickly to a Black-out

SCENE 3

The same. Later that evening

The room is as Vernon and the others left it

Jackie (*off, hardly audible*) D'you wanna go through? All right? Just go through.

The hall light is switched on

(*Off, more audibly*) Ooh, it's all dark.

Jackie enters, wearing a fur jacket and carrying her handbag and a bottle of whisky. She puts on the main light

Muhammad enters

What's going on? (*She puts the bottle on the table*) Had some friends over.

Muhammad leans against the wall, Jackie puts on the lamp on the wall-unit and goes into the hall

She exits towards Vernon's room

(*Off*) Vernon! (*She knocks on Vernon's door*) Vernon.

Muhammad sits at the table

Jackie comes back into the room, takes off her jacket and puts it on the sofa

You all right?
Muhammad In car; in taxi; in, er . . .
Jackie Mm. Got a bit car-sick?
Muhammad Er . . . (*He gestures above his head, meaning "aeroplane"*)

Jackie Yeh, 't's really smoky.
Muhammad Er ... no good.

Jackie goes to the bar and switches on the lamp there

Jackie D'you want a whisky? Whisky?
Muhammad La. [No.]

Jackie pours herself a whisky and water

Jackie (*indicating the sofa*) D'you want to come and sit over here? It's nice and comfortable. Come and sit over here.
Muhammad I come?
Jackie Yeh.

Muhammad crosses slowly to the sofa. He coughs once on the way

Muhammad (*as he crosses*) Ismāh-ly. [Forgive me.]
Jackie Mm. Yeh. You sure you don't want a whisky?
Muhammad La.
Jackie D'you want a glass of water? A glass of water?
Muhammad Water.
Jackie (*going to the bar*) Yeh, all right. I'll get you some. 'T's best thing, you know, if you're feeling a bit sick. Flush your system out. I hope Vernon gets back soon. 'T's my flatmate. (*She hands him a glass of water*) Here y'are. 'E 'asn't really met any of my friends. Be good when 'e comes back and sees you 'ere. That'll give 'im a shock. I bet 'e's never met an oil sheikh before. (*She lights a cigarette*) D'you want a cigarette? Cigarette?
Muhammad OK.

Jackie gives him a cigarette and lights it for him

Jackie All right? (*She sits down*)

Pause

Muhammad Where this?
Jackie What?
Muhammad Where ... this?
Jackie Here? This is my flat, yeh? 'T's where I live.
Muhammad No London?
Jackie Yeh, it's London. 'T's Dollis Hill.
Muhammad Big, big.
Jackie Oh yeh, it's two-bedroomed, you know.

Muhammad finishes the water

D'you want another one?

Muhammad does not understand

D'you want some more water?

Muhammad makes a vague, affirmative gesture

Yeh, all right, I'll get you some.

Jackie goes to the bar, and pours the water. Muhammad stubs out the cigarette in an ashtray

Muhammad Excuse. (*He coughs*)
Jackie Here you are. I'll stick it down here, all right? (*She puts the glass on the floor beside him*)
Muhammad Ismāh-ly. [Forgive me.] Make, er ... Where?
Jackie What?
Muhammad Water.
Jackie It's down there, yeh? It's on the floor.
Muhammad OK. (*He picks it up slowly*)

Pause

Jackie 'Ow long you been over here?
Muhammad Excuse?
Jackie 'Ow long 'ave you been in London?
Muhammad London, big, big.
Jackie Yeh. You over 'ere on business?
Muhammad Business, business.
Jackie What sort of business you doing over 'ere? Is it deals with BP and that, yeh?
Muhammad Business ma'a [with] Abdullah.
Jackie Oh, you do business with Abdullah?
Muhammad Business ma'a Abdullah.
Jackie Yeh.
Muhammad Wa [and] Ibrahim; you know?
Jackie Yeh ...
Muhammad Wa Marwan. You know him?
Jackie Yeh ... No. No, I know Abdullah. Abdullah is a very old friend of mine. I have known him for a year.
Muhammad Abdullah come here?
Jackie No, he's not coming here.

Pause

Muhammad Where girl?
Jackie What?
Muhammad Where, er ... Albanāt hadoleech? [Those other girls?]
Jackie I don't understand.
Muhammad Where girl? Where? Is er—you, is girl, girl, girl, girl, girl.
Jackie Oh, girls, yeh? No, I told you, I don't share with girls. I share with a gentleman friend of mine, Vernon. We're just good friends.
Muhammad No, friend. Marwan, he my brother.
Jackie Oh, really?
Muhammad Ibrahim, he my, mm, family ...
Jackie Yeh.
Muhammad Er ... business.
Jackie Oh, it's family business, yeh?

Muhammad Business.
Jackie Oh, it's good, you know. Means you can trust people. No-one's gonna do you.
Muhammad Important.
Jackie Is it very big deals, yeh?
Muhammad London.
Jackie Yeh, I really want Vernon to meet you, you know. D'you meet a lot of other millionaires and tycoons and that?

Muhammad does not understand

What sort of business are you setting up in London? Is it very big oil deals?
Muhammad Sheriket es-Sālim. [Sālim and Company.]

Pause

Jackie Yeh.

Pause

Cheers!
Muhammad Excuse?
Jackie Cheers.
Muhammad Cheers?
Jackie Yeh.
Muhammad (*patting the sofa*) Is good!
Jackie What?
Muhammad Is good.
Jackie Oh, yeh, it's lovely—it's nice and comfortable.
Muhammad In my country, many, many English cheers.
Jackie Oh, really? D'you buy a lot of them over there?
Muhammad Is, er—Arads.
Jackie Arabs?
Muhammad Arads.
Jackie I don't understand.
Muhammad Is Arads' cheers. Is, er, Arads, is shop, Arads.
Jackie 'Arrods!
Muhammad Arads.
Jackie Oh, yeh, that's nice. D'you shop there?
Muhammad Is shop.
Jackie 'T's a nice shop, you know—it's very classy.
Muhammad Is shop.
Jackie I buy my make-up there, you know, perfume and that.
Muhammad Is shop.
Jackie Yeh.

Pause

Is your brother in the hotel with you?
Muhammad Excuse?
Jackie Is your brother staying with you, in the hotel?

Muhammad Hotel *Royal Garden.*
Jackie Oh, really . . . ? Yeh, it's a nice hotel, you know? I have been there.
Muhammad You, er—la. [No.]
Jackie What?
Muhammad You, er—no.
Jackie Look, I'm telling you: I've been there.
Muhammad La. Er, manty fāh'ma. [Er, you don't understand.]
Jackie Look: I have been to the *Royal Garden Hotel.* For drinks, y'know?
Cocktails, actually.
Muhammad You English?
Jackie Yeh.
Muhammad No American?
Jackie No.
Muhammad OK.

Pause

(*Pointing at the television*) Video?
Jackie No, it's a television.
Muhammad Television ma'a [with] video?
Jackie No.
Muhammad OK.

Pause

What your name?
Jackie Jackie.
Muhammad Excuse?
Jackie Jackie, yeh?
Muhammad Jackie-yeh.
Jackie No. Jackie. Like Jackie Kennedy, you know? Onassis?
Muhammad (*none the wiser*) OK.

Pause. Jackie goes to the bar

Jackie D'you want a drink yet? Yeh? D'you want a whisky? Whisky?
Muhammad Whisky.
Jackie Yeh, all right.
Muhammad Oh, is, er . . .
Jackie What's the matter?
Muhammad Is, er . . .
Jackie This? 'T's a bar, yeh? It's nice. Not many people have got one of
these.
Muhammad (*getting up*) OK. (*He goes to the bar, where he takes out a thick
wad of money*) Hādha bkem? [How much is it?]
Jackie What?
Muhammad Er, er, take, er, take . . .
Jackie What's that for? You don't have to pay for it. No! (*She walks
away from the bar*)

Muhammad is puzzled, and puts the money away

My friend'll probably be back soon.
Muhammad Excuse?
Jackie My friend, will be back soon. Soon.
Muhammad Soon?
Jackie Yeh.
Muhammad Inshallah. [Allah willing.] (*He gulps down his whisky quickly, in one go*) OK. Er . . . where . . . hammām? [toilet?]
Jackie What?
Muhammad Where, er, where . . .
Jackie 'T's the matter? D'you want the toilet? Toilet?
Muhammad Toilet, OK.
Jackie Yeh, all right, I'll show you.

She takes him out into the hall

Will you come round? Come through, yeh? 'T's down there. Right down that way. No, go on straight down the bottom. That's it. Yeh. (*She comes back into the room*)

Pause

Muhammad (*coming back into the room*) Excuse. Er . . . ibreeg, [jug of water,] er . . . water . . . make . . .
Jackie D'you want the bathroom? Bathroom?
Muhammad Make . . .
Jackie Yeh, it's round there, through that door round there.
Muhammad OK.
Jackie All right.

Muhammad goes out of one door and back in through the other. Jackie goes into the hall and points towards the bathroom. Muhammad follows her

No, not there, look, round here, yeh, next to the toilet? That one, yeh. That's it. (*She comes back into the room*)
Muhammad (*following her*) Excuse . . . em—ibreeg. [jug of water.]
Jackie Don't understand.
Muhammad Ibreeg . . . wallah . . . [Jug of water . . . by Allah] make, er . . . water. Make, er . . .
Jackie D'you want a glass of water, yeh? A glass of water? (*She points to the water-jug*)

Muhammad attempts to pick up the jug. She takes it

'T's all right, I'll pour it out for you. (*She pours him a glass of water, and holds it out to him*)

Muhammad takes the jug, and goes out of the room with it

(*Following him*) What's the matter? No, you don't want that. Can I have that back, please? Where are you taking that?

Muhammad exits to the toilet with the jug

Jackie pauses for a moment, then goes back into the lounge, perplexed. She puts on the record left on the turntable by Vernon, then sits down. Pause. The toilet flushes, off. She regains her composure

Muhammad enters

Are you all right?
Muhammad OK.
Jackie What 'ave you done with the jug?
Muhammad OK.
Jackie What, have you done, with the water-jug?
Muhammad OK.
Jackie (*getting up*) Jesus! What's 'e done with it?

Jackie rushes past Muhammad, and exits to the toilet

Muhammad (*following her into the hall*) I come now?

Once out of the room, Muhammad goes the other way, not having seen which way Jackie went

(*Off*) Where he go? Excuse. Excuse. (*He knocks on Jackie's bedroom door*)

Jackie enters with the jug. She almost smells inside it, but doesn't quite. She shudders. She puts it back on the bar. She is disgusted

Muhammad enters

OK. Excuse. Is many, many, er, make, er . . .
Jackie Look, when we was in the pub, did Abdullah explain to you why you was comin' 'ere?
Muhammad Excuse?
Jackie Did Abdullah explain to you, *you*, why *you* was comin' 'ere? *Here.*

She points downwards, to the ground, as it were; but she happens to be standing over the sofa, and Muhammad therefore takes "here" to refer specifically to the sofa

Muhammad Here?
Jackie Yeh.
Muhammad OK, understand. Excuse!

Muhammad crosses to the sofa. Jackie moves away from it

Jackie Just better to be straight, you know?
Muhammad (*indicating the sofa*) Here?
Jackie Yeh.

Muhammad gestures to indicate that Jackie should remove the ashtray and the dish of nuts from the sofa

Muhammad OK, er, make, er . . .

Jackie does nothing

OK, ana asawweeha! [I'll do it myself!] (*He puts the things on the side-table, muttering*) Ēsh hal warta! Ēsh hal warta! ala kull hāl . . .[1]

---

[1] What a situation! What a situation! Anyway . . .

Jackie What's the matter? You all right?

He stands, waiting for her to sit with him on the sofa. He gestures to that effect. Pause. She does not join him. Eventually, he sits down. Pause

Got a car in London?
Muhammad Excuse?
Jackie Do you drive a car?
Muhammad Car . . .
Jackie Yeh? In London
Muhammad Taxi, no good. (*He indicates his stomach*)
Jackie Oh, yeh, no, no, I mean—have you got a car? In your country . . .
Muhammad In my country . . .
Jackie Do you drive a car?
Muhammad Car? Many, many.
Jackie Oh, really?
Muhammad In my country is er, Pontiac, is Cadillac, is Toyota, is Datsun, is Mercedes, is Rolls-Royce.
Jackie You got a Rolls-Royce, yeh?
Muhammad Many, many.
Jackie (*miming driving*) You got a chauffeur? You got a *chauffeur*?
Muhammad You? La. [No.]
Jackie What?
Muhammad You—er, no.
Jackie Yeh, I drive.
Muhammad La!
Jackie I do. I've got a driving licence.
Muhammad In my country, is, er, mm . . . (*indicating himself*) make, er, car: er . . . girl, la.
Jackie Don't girls drive?

Muhammad tuts

Why not?
Muhammad (*tutting*) Hādha suāl mustaheel. [This is an impossible question.]

Long pause

Jackie D'you want a cigarette?
Muhammad OK.

While Jackie is lighting his cigarette, Muhammad holds her wrist

Jackie No, 't's all right. What sort of places have you been to in London?
Muhammad Excuse?
Jackie Been to any clubs? Clubs.
Muhammad Club! I go club.
Jackie Oh. There's a lot of nice clubs in London. I'll tell you what: we'll go to a nice club next week, yeh? Have a nice meal, you know? Steak an' champagne an' that, yeh?
Muhammad Excuse?

Jackie You and me. YOU, will take ME.
Muhammad Now?
Jackie No, not now, no. Next week, yeh?
Muhammad OK. Inshallah. [If Allah wills.]

Pause

What him?
Jackie What?
Muhammad What him?
Jackie This? 'T's my brooch, yeh? Brooch? 'T's nice, yeh. D'you like it?
Muhammad What him?
Jackie It's cherries. Cherries, what you eat?
Muhammad You eat him?
Jackie Yeh. 'T's nice. D'you wanna 'ave a look?
Muhammad Ajeeb . . . [Strange . . .]
Jackie All right, I'll show you. (*She takes off the brooch*) There you are.
   'S pretty, yeh? Pretty? (*She gives it to him*) D'you like it?
Muhammad Shukran. [Thank you.]
Jackie Yeh, it's nice.
Muhammad Eat him. (*He puts the brooch in his mouth*)
Jackie No, you don't eat 'em. No, they're not real, just pretend, you know.
Muhammad OK. Shukran. [Thank you.] (*He puts it in his pocket*)
Jackie I'm not giving them to you. 'T's not a present. (*After a pause*) Can
   I have my brooch back, please?
Muhammad Ajeeb! [Strange!]
Jackie Come on. Yeh?
Muhammad OK.
Jackie All right—come on.

He gets up. He pulls out the wad of money, and offers it to her

What's that? I don't want that, I want my brooch back, yeh, I don't
want—I want my brooch.
Muhammad Hādha bkem? [How much is it?]
Jackie In your pocket.
Muhammad Na'am. Hādha bkem? [Yes. How much is it?]
Jackie My brooch. Yeh? Yeh.

He gets out the brooch. She snatches it from his hand

Thank you. I don't want that. (*She puts on the brooch, using one of the
mirrors on the wall*)
Muhammad Oh, er, excuse.
Jackie Yeh.
Muhammad Understand. Is, er . . . you make . . . mm; I make—mm; al
floos [the money] is . . . make, excuse. (*He sits down. He is extremely
angry with himself. He tuts*) H'maar akmak! Kaif irtakabt mithil
hal-khata? Ismāh-ly.[2] Excuse.

---

[2] Donkey! Idiot! How could you make such a mistake? Forgive me.

Jackie Yeh, all right. (*She sits down*)

Muhammad takes out a tube of Refreshers, a tube of Fruit Gums, and some worry-beads. He offers her a sweet

Muhammad OK?
Jackie What's that? Fruit Gums? No, I don't want one.

He puts a Refresher in his mouth, and puts the sweets and worry-beads away. Pause. Then he flicks cigarette ash on the floor

D'you want an ashtray, yeh? (*She gets him an ashtray, and goes to the bar*) Use an ashtray, don't flick ash on the carpet, you know, it's a nice rug. D'you want one? D'you want a whisky?
Muhammad OK.

Jackie pours out the whiskies, just stopping herself from using the jug. She uses the soda-syphon instead

Jackie (*looking at her watch*) 'Ere y'are. All right? Yeh, Vernon'll be back soon. 'E's 'ad some friends over tonight for a party. Yeh, 'e's probably taken them on to a club, you know, they've gone dancing. Dancing.
Muhammad Dance?
Jackie Yeh.
Muhammad You dance?
Jackie What?
Muhammad Er, dance?
Jackie D'you wanna dance?
Muhammad Dance?
Jackie Yeh, all right.
Muhammad OK?
Jackie Yeh.
Muhammad OK. (*He settles back comfortably*) Mumtāz! [Excellent!]
Jackie What's the matter?
Muhammad Make, akthar. [Make, more/faster.]
Jackie Well, come on, you dance an' all, yeh?
Muhammad U ba'ad? [What happens next?]
Jackie No, I'm not dancing on my own!
Muhammad Make, urugsi! [Make, dance!]
Jackie No, I feel stupid. (*She sits down*)
Muhammad Make, er . . .
Jackie Look, I'll dance with you, you know? I don't want to dance on me own.
Muhammad OK, er . . . (*He takes out the money*) OK?
Jackie What's that?
Muhammad Urugseely! [Dance for me!]
Jackie What?
Muhammad Urugsi! [Dance!] (*He proceeds to peel off notes, one by one on to the sofa*)
Jackie What's that for, yeh?
Muhammad (*peeling off another note*) Dance? (*Another*) Dance?

Jackie Yeh, look—I'll dance with you!

Muhammad (*another note*) Dance?

Jackie I don't understand.

Muhammad Understand! (*Another note*) Understand.

Jackie No, I don't.

Muhammad OK, more. More; more? More; more; more. (*He continues to peel off notes*)

Jackie Is that a present, yeh?

Muhammad More?

Jackie Are you giving that to me?

Muhammad OK? OK. (*He throws all the peeled-off notes on the floor*) Urugsi. [Dance.]

Jackie I'll take it!

Muhammad Take, er make, urugsi . . .

Jackie I'm gonna take it, you know?

Muhammad Take. Take, take!

Jackie What, is it a present, yeh?

Muhammad Urugsi, urugsi.

Jackie I'm gonna take it.

Muhammad Take, take, take, take.

Jackie All right. (*She picks it all up*) I've taken it.

Muhammad OK, make, er . . . dance.

Jackie I'll dance with you!

Muhammad More?

Jackie No.

Muhammad More!

Jackie No!

He starts throwing more notes across the floor

What's that? I'm not picking it up down there.

Muhammad More?

Jackie No.

Muhammad More? More . . .

Jackie I'll dance with you, you know? We'll dance together——

Muhammad More?

Jackie —all right?

Muhammad OK?

Jackie Yeh.

Muhammad OK.

Jackie Right. Come on, then. Come on. (*She gets up, and takes his hand*)

He gets up

That's it.

Muhammad OK, now?

Jackie Yeh.

Muhammad OK. (*He pushes her down on to the sofa*)

Jackie What's the matter?

Muhammad OK, make, er—el-treek; [the lights;] OK, em . . . (*He puts out the main light*)
Jackie What're you doing?
Muhammad OK, OK, make, er make . . .
Jackie (*getting up*) No, look, leave the lights on yeh?
Muhammad OK . . .
Jackie Look, Vernon'll be back soon, yeh?
Muhammad (*grabbing her*) OK.
Jackie Will you stop pushing me?

He pushes her back on to the sofa

What's the matter with you?
Muhammad Tsallakhy . . . [Become naked/Get undressed . . .]
Jackie (*getting up*) Right. I'm gonna turn the lights on.
Muhammad La—khalleeha el-treek. [No—leave the lights off.]
Jackie Look: you leave the lights on, d'you understand? On. All right?
(*She switches on the main light*)

Muhammad
Jackie } (*together*) { La . . . make, em.
No, you don't touch them, you know? D'you understand?

Muhammad OK. Mā dām, you, el-treek.[3] Understand.
Jackie Right?
Muhammad OK, OK.
Jackie Yeh. You don't touch them, yeh?
Muhammad OK, make, er . . .
Jackie Yeh.
Muhammad OK . . . (*He pats the sofa for her to join him*) OK.
Jackie Yeh, all right. You leave them alone. (*She sits with him*) It's just that my friend'll be back soon.
Muhammad Soon?
Jackie Yeh.
Muhammad Inshallah. [If Allah wills.] (*He settles back resignedly*)

Pause

Jackie Did you buy any clothes when you went to Oxford Street?
Muhammad Excuse?
Jackie When you went to Oxford Street, yeh? Did you buy any clothes? *Clothes.* (*She demonstrates by touching his jacket*)
Muhammad Clothes!
Jackie Yeh, d'you understand?
Muhammad Clothes! OK! Understand! Clothes: it mean "Hadoum". (*He stands up, and removes his jacket*) Make, el-treek, [the lights,] mm, OK . . .

He starts turning out the lights again. Jackie follows him, turning them back on

---

[3] If it's you, the lights. (Since it's you, I'll allow the lights to go on.)

Jackie No, look, I've told you, you leave the lights on, yeh? Listen: when we was in the pub, Abdullah told you you was just comin' back with me to meet a few friends of mine, and 'ave some nice drinks, you know?

Muhammad OK. Khallās.⁴ (*He picks up the whole telephone, and holds out the receiver to Jackie*) OK. Er . . . make him Abdullah.

Jackie I don't know his number.

Muhammad Make him Abdullah.

Jackie I don't know his phone number.

Muhammad No?

Jackie No.

Muhammad OK. (*He puts back the telephone*)

Pause

(*Muttering*) Ēsh hal warta [What a situation] . . . OK.

He attempts to take back the money, which Jackie is still holding

Jackie No. No, you gave it to me, yeh?—it's a present. A deal's a deal, you know?—you don't make an agreement, and then back out of it.

Muhammad OK, dance?

Jackie Yeh, I'll dance with *you*!

Muhammad Dance?

Jackie Yeh.

Muhammad Il humdillah, OK! [Allah be praised, OK!] OK, make er, make er, dance, OK?

Jackie Come on, then, come on. You come and dance an' all, you know?

Muhammad Mumtaz! [Excellent!] OK, akthar! [OK, faster/more!] (*He sits at the table*)

Jackie I'm not dancing on me own, yeh?

Muhammad OK, urugsi, urugseely, [dance, dance for me], make, er make—OK, make, er dance, make, er OK, take er, OK, tsallakhy! Tayyib! [get undressed! Good!] OK! Urugsi! Urugseely! Hadoum!! [Dance! Dance for me! Clothes!!] (*He opens the whisky left on the table by Jackie. He looks for a clean glass on the table, smelling them*)

Jackie What's the matter, d'you want your glass, yeh? Here you are, here's your glass, all right?

Muhammad OK, you er . . . (*He pulls her on to his knee*)

Jackie (*friendly*) What're you doing?

Muhammad OK, tsallakhy! [OK, get undressed!] (*He pulls at her clothes*)

Jackie (*jumping off*) No, leave that. Look, we don't pull people's clothes, you know? Gentlemen don't do that in England!

Muhammad Er, make belly . . .

Jackie What?

Muhammad Make belly-dance.

Jackie Ballet? I don't do ballet!

Muhammad Make him, make, er, OK, mumtaz! [excellent!]

---

⁴ It is the end. (This is the giddy limit/This is just about as much as I can take.)

He pats her bottom. She revolves

Jackie What're you doing, yeh?
Muhammad OK, akthar, [faster/more,] make, er—mumtaz! [excellent!]
Jackie No, I can't keep turning round in circles!

She is turning round in circles. He continues to pat her bottom

Muhammad OK. Akthar! [Faster/more!]
Jackie (*not unfriendly*) What you doin', yeh? Don't be stupid.

Frankie enters

Oh, hi.

Muhammad seizes Frankie's arm

Muhammad OK, two?
Frankie Hey! D'you mind?

Frankie runs out

Jackie No, it's all right, yeh—(*she**Frankie** (*off*) Vernon! There's a
starts to pursue Frankie*)—no, no,   bloke in there tried to grab hold
it's all right! (*She remembers the*   of my arm!
money on the floor and rushes back
to pick it all up)
Muhammad (*to Jackie*) Is OK, is, er, more . . .

Vernon, Frankie and Irving enter

Vernon What's going on?
Jackie Oh, hi, Ver.
Vernon Who's this?
Jackie No, it's all right, 'e's a friend of mine.
Vernon Strange sort of friend—she says he just grabbed her arm.
Frankie That's right.
Jackie Oh, no. No, 'e was just tryin' to give 'er a drink, you know?
Frankie Well, it's a queer way of going about it.
Jackie Yeh, well, 'e don't understand. I think she was a bit funny with 'im.
Frankie Look: he grabbed hold of my coat!
Jackie No, 'e didn't.
Frankie 'E did!
Vernon All right, Frankie!
Irving Have you been molesting my wife?
Vernon Irving!
Frankie This isn't Jackie, is it?
Vernon Of course it's Jackie! Jackie Scragg, Frankie Gammon. Irving
Gammon.
Irving Evening.
Jackie Hi.
Frankie Jesus Christ!

Frankie exits to hang up her coat

Jackie discreetly stuffs the money in her bag

Muhammad OK? OK. (*To Vernon*) You go. (*To Irving*) You go.
Irving What!
Vernon Jackie, who is this character?

Frankie enters

Jackie It's all right, Vern, yeh? Vernon: I'd like you to meet a friend of
mine, Mohammed. (*This is how she pronounces his name*) He's in London,
doing some very important big business deals.
Vernon Mohammed?
Jackie Yeh.
Vernon Jesus Christ! *A bloody Arab!!!*

BLACK-OUT

ACT II

The same. A few minutes later

The light in the kitchen is now on. Frankie is sitting on a bar-stool. Irving is lurking about. Muhammad and Jackie are standing together

Jackie What's the matter? Your tie? It's all right. (*She adjusts his tie*) That's it. All right?

Muhammad OK. Soon? Soon?

Frankie Soon he'll be all right.

Jackie D'you want to come and sit down, yeh? 'Ave a little whisky? Whisky? (*She sits down*)

Muhammad (*sitting down*) La. [No.]

Irving No, they're not allowed to drink, you know. That's why they come over here.

Vernon enters; he puts on the apron, and proceeds to clear the table

Frankie How do you know?

Irving Well, it's their religion, isn't it?

Jackie He does; he drinks whisky.

Irving Does he? Naughty boy! You'll get the cane!

Frankie Stupid bugger!

Jackie (*to Muhammad*) No, it's all right, don't take any notice of him, yeh?—he's joking. It's a joke.

Vernon Was that a joke, Irving?

Irving No, I'm serious. They get their hands chopped off, as well.

Frankie Irving!

Jackie No, they don't.

Irving They do; I've seen it on the telly.

Pause

It's very nice to meet you . . . Jackie. I've heard a lot about you.

Jackie Oh, really?

Vernon exits to the kitchen

Irving Quite surprised to see you, really. I should've thought in your line, it was pretty well an all-night job.

Jackie Well, it is, yeh. I just finished early tonight.

Irving I should've thought Saturday was the big night?

Jackie Oh, yeh, it's very busy on Saturdays, lot of heavy action.

Irving Lot of people there, eh?

Jackie Oh, yeh, get a few punters in, y'know, sort of eleven-deep round the tables tonight, Manhattan skyline.

Frankie Oh, yes?

Irving Lot of money flying about, eh?

Jackie Yeh, a few pennies to spend, you know?

Irving (*leaning across Jackie to reach the ashtray*) Excuse me.

Jackie 'T's all right.

Vernon enters with a tea-tray. He continues to clear the table

Vernon Where does this character spring from, Jackie? What's his country of origin?

Jackie He's an Arab, yeh? From Saudi Arabia.

Frankie Oh, Arabia?

Muhammad Saudi Arabia.

Jackie It's your country.

Muhammad In my country.

Frankie That's nice.

Jackie Yeh, 'e's over here settin' up oil deals an' that.

Vernon Oh, is he?

Irving They're really wealthy, aren't they?

Jackie Oh, yeh, they walk in the club and cash up a few grand without thinkin' about it, you know?

Irving Yeh, they go in for a lot of gambling.

Jackie Oh, yeh. Yeh, well, it's relaxation for 'em, innit? D'you go gamin'?

Vernon exits to the kitchen with the tray

Irving How d'you mean? Oh, gaming? Yeh, well . . . a bit—you know.

Jackie Yeh, you've got to 'ave the money to spend, 'aven't you?

Irving No, it's not that. Don't get the time. Don't get into the West End very much.

Frankie What you talking about? Course we do.

Irving When?

Frankie Saturday nights.

Irving Yes . . . go and see a film occasionally.

Jackie What sort of clubs d'you go to, then?

Irving Um . . .

Pause

Frankie Different ones.

Frankie exits to join Vernon in the kitchen

Irving Forgotten, really, um . . . been to a few with friends. Haven't been to yours, though.

Jackie 'T's a nice club, you know? There's a lot of big money goin' about.

Irving I shall have to come in and see you some time.

Jackie Yeh . . . well, we're not allowed to talk to people when we're working, you know? They're very strict about that.

Irving No chance of a few free chips, then, eh?

Jackie Oh, no.

Vernon enters, followed by Frankie

Vernon Who's this friend of his that you know, then, Jackie?
Jackie Oh, 'e's a very old friend of mine.
Vernon Oh, yes? Who's that?
Jackie He's called Abdullah.
Vernon Abdullah?
Jackie Mm.
Vernon Jesus Christ! Another one!
Muhammad You know Abdullah?
Vernon No, I don't know Abdullah!

Vernon exits to the kitchen

Jackie No, 'e don't know 'im, 'e's just a friend of mine.
Muhammad (*to Frankie*) You know Abdullah?
Frankie (*going towards the hall*) Ooh, no, I don't know him either.

Vernon enters

Vernon (*as he enters*) Get out the way, Frankie! (*He continues to clear the table*)
Muhammad (*to Irving*) You know Abdullah?
Irving What?
Jackie No, 'e's just my friend, yeh?
Irving How long you been there, then?
Jackie What?
Irving In your present position, if you'll pardon the expression. (*He laughs uproariously*)
Jackie Oh, just a few months—well, I'll probably sort of move on later in the year, you know, go and work abroad an' that.
Frankie Oh, really?
Jackie Oh, yeh, if you're London-trained you can go anywhere in the world.
Frankie Can you?
Jackie Yeh, I could go to Amsterdam, you know, you can pick up about five hundred a week over there.
Frankie That's a lot of money, isn't it?

Vernon has now completely cleared up. He exits to the kitchen

Jackie Yeh, it is. I might go to Africa, an' all, you know. Nigeria—get a lot of big punters over there.
Frankie You'll have to get inoculated.

Frankie exits to the kitchen

Jackie (*calling after her*) Yeh, I know. I will.

During the following speech, Frankie discreetly returns and closes the dining-area door, then goes back to Vernon in the kitchen

Might go to the States an' all, you know: Atlantic City's gone legal.

Irving Yeh, I thought it probably would.

Jackie Picked up forty million in the first week.

Irving Oh, easily, easily.

Jackie Quite a few of us go and work on the cruisers an' all, you know— I might go to Miami and the Bahamas an' that, go on the *QE2*, ah, it's everyone's dream to work on that boat, you know, it's lovely.

Irving You must lead a really exciting life.

Jackie Yeh—you meet a lot of people.

Irving Pity you can't talk to them—eh? (*He laughs uproariously*)

Jackie Not really.

Irving Get to know them. (*He gets up, and looks through the open lounge door in the general direction of the kitchen*)

Jackie Don't really want to, actually. To be quite honest, it don't pay to get too involved, you know; I know that don't sound very nice, but you can get it thrown back in your face.

Muhammad OK, go?

Irving What?

Muhammad You, er, go?

Irving Go?!

Jackie (*to Muhammad*) What, no, it's all right, he's just having a drink, yeh? (*To Irving*) D'you work with Vern, then?

Irving That's right. Yeh. (*He sits down*)

Jackie Oh, really, how's it goin', you sellin'?

Irving Oh, yes, it's going really well, you know.

Jackie Yeh?

Irving We've had a lot of orders in recently, specially since the Metro came in.

Jackie 'T's right.

Irving It's aroused a lot of interest in Leyland in general.

Muhammad Excuse . . .

Irving What?

Jackie Yeh, it's a nice little car, you know?

During the following, Muhammad gets up, and peers towards the kitchen through the clear window-pane in the closed door

Irving It is, yeh; have you tried it?

Jackie No, I haven't, no.

Irving Oh, well, you'll have to come in for a test-drive, won't you?

Jackie Yeh . . . yeh, I might.

Irving Don't tell Vernon, though, eh?

Jackie Why not?

Irving Well, he might think I was poaching, mightn't he?

Jackie I don't see why.

Muhammad stands by the open door

Muhammad OK, go now.

Irving What?

Muhammad You make, er . . . go.

Jackie No, it's all right, he's just havin' a drink, yeh?

Irving Look, excuse me; I'm just having a chat with this young lady here.

Jackie Just come and sit down, have a nice little whisky, all right?

Irving It's funny you being brunette, you know; I thought you'd have red hair.

Jackie Oh, did you?

Irving Yeh.

Muhammad Here this, er, mm—girl. Is, er . . . here, is, er . . . barman ma'a [with] girl, make, er, like this. (*He claps together vertical cupped hands*)

Irving (*getting up*) Eh?

Muhammad Is here, you, make, er, em . . .

Irving I'm not going anywhere—right?

Irving exits to the kitchen

Muhammad closes the door behind him

Muhammad OK.

Jackie (*standing up*) What's the matter? Come and sit down, yeh? Have a whisky. Whisky?

Muhammad OK. (*He sits down in the centre of the sofa*)

Jackie pours him a whisky

Frankie enters, a bit flustered, followed by Irving. She goes to her bag and adjusts her make-up

Irving stands in the doorway, surveying the scene, then closes the door and exits to join Vernon in the kitchen

Both doors are now closed. Muhammad is extremely confused

Jackie (*giving the whisky to Muhammad*) There you are. All right?

Muhammad La!

Jackie 'S the matter? I just got it for you.

Loud mirth from the kitchen

All right? I'll just stick it on 'ere, yeh? (*She puts the drink on the table*)— you can 'elp yourself when you feel like it. (*She sits down beside him*)

Frankie finishes her make-up and moves across to the sofa

Frankie Quite nice-looking, really, isn't he?

Jackie Oh, yeh, well, they are, you know—get a lot of 'em in the club.

Frankie Not too dark.

Jackie No. Well, they are quite dark, you know? It's a really hot country, where they live.

Frankie (*sitting on the other side of Muhammad*) Yes, I know that.

Pause

Sweet little beard, isn't it?

Jackie Yeh, it's nice. I don't usually like beards, you know?—I don't like them when they're all over your face—that one's all right.

Frankie Yes, it's neat, isn't it?
Jackie Yeh.
Frankie Oh, hasn't he got nice eyes?
Jackie Yeh, lovely.
Frankie Mm. Dark.
Jackie Mm.
Frankie He's a bit like Omar Sharif, isn't he?
Jackie Yeh, he is, you know? I like him; he's really mysterious.
Frankie Mind you, he's a bit overweight.
Jackie I don't know . . . I don't mind if it's spread out. Not like English blokes, drink beer all the time, pot bellies, it's 'orrible.
Frankie Well, he's got a pot, hasn't he?
Jackie No, not really.
Frankie (*pointing*) Well, what's that, then?

Muhammad places his hands over his crutch

Still, at least he hasn't got one of those things on.
Jackie What's that?
Frankie You know—sheets.
Jackie Oh, no, they don't wear them; not when they're doing business, anyway: they wear really nice suits, you know—really expensive.
Frankie (*feeling Muhammad's lapel*) Well, you can see this is good quality, isn't it?
Jackie (*feeling the other lapel*) Yeh, it's lovely.
Muhammad (*proceeding to remove his jacket*) OK.
Jackie No, it's all right! Have your drink, yeh? (*She hands him his glass*) Whisky?
Muhammad Whisky, OK. (*He takes the glass*)
Jackie Cheers.
Frankie Cheers.
Muhammad (*patting the sofa*) Is good, cheers.

Vernon and Irving enter through the lounge-area door and go to the bar

Muhammad immediately puts his whisky on Jackie's lap

Jackie What's the matter?

Vernon Everything goes wrong with your car, Irving.
Irving It's not my fault, is it?
Vernon Of course it's your fault.
Irving It's the workshop, I mean, they don't check 'em up properly before they send 'em out.
Vernon They check 'em out, it's you —it's the way you drive them, Irving.
Irving No, if they'd check 'em properly, they'd find out if it was a rogue car, wouldn't they?

Frankie Would you pass the ashtray, please, Jackie?
Jackie Oh. All right. (*She passes the ashtray to Frankie. To Muhammad*) What's the matter?

Muhammad says nothing

Frankie Could you pass the nuts over as well, please?

Jackie passes the nuts to Frankie

Jackie (*to Muhammad*) D'you want

Vernon Not a rogue car, it's a rogue driver. . . .

Irving Come on, Vernon, don't exaggerate. I mean, it's hardly my fault if the lock on the hatchback goes, is it?

Vernon It's always something, Irving—all these little things, they mount up.

Irving It's like the carburettor. It's only going to be a fifteen-minute job, isn't it? Little twiddle with a screwdriver and it's done, eh?

Vernon It's always you, though, isn't it?

Jackie Can I have the ashtray, Vernon. (*She takes it*)

Vernon D'you want a drink, Jackie?

Jackie No, it's all right, I've got one.

Vernon (*picking up the whisky bottle*) Where did this come from, Jackie?

Jackie Oh, it's a really nice whisky, you know. Mohammed brought it.

Vernon Did he?

Jackie Yeh.

Vernon D'you want some, Mohammed? Whisky. Whisky?

Muhammad La. [No.]

Frankie Na. He doesn't, Ver.

Jackie Stick it down 'ere, all right? (*She puts down the ashtray*)

Irving Stick it where you like, eh? (*He laughs uproariously*)

Vernon How about you, Frankie?

Frankie Gin and tonic, please.

Vernon Gin and tonic for the lady! (*He pours her a drink*)

Jackie Here y'are; 'ere's your drink.

Muhammad tuts

'T's the matter?

Vernon Ice, Frankie?

Frankie Please.

Pause. Frankie utters her noise, q.v.

Muhammad Excuse?

Frankie Eh?

Pause. Muhammad takes some nuts from the dish in Frankie's lap

Vernon Here we are, Frankie. (*He hands her a drink*)

Frankie Thank you.

Vernon Oh, glad to see you've got your appetite back.

Frankie Mm . . . just a bit.

Irving Yeh, well, she's not eaten for half an hour, has she, eh?

Frankie There's no need to be rude, Irving.

Vernon Don't listen to him, Frankie. Enjoy that cheesecake, did you?

some nuts, yeh? D'you want some peanuts?

Frankie No; no, he doesn't.

Jackie I'll just get an ashtray, actually. (*She goes to the bar*)

Frankie I did, thank you—it was a super meal, Vernon.

Jackie What d'you 'ave?

Frankie (*defensively*) Steak . . .

Jackie Oh, did you?

Irving Nice and juicy, mine was.

Frankie (*defensively*) So was mine.

Vernon They had T-bone steaks, these two.

Jackie Oh, really? I can never manage to get through one of them, you know?

Vernon They had T-bone steaks with garnish; french fries, peas, grilled tomatoes . . .

Irving Didn't have mushrooms, though, did they?

Vernon No, they didn't have mushrooms, did they, Irving? But you do get mushrooms at the Berni, don't you?

Irving That's right, you do—hand-picked.

Vernon Something else new I've learnt this evening . . . Then they had prawn cocktails with roll-and-butter to start with. Then, seven different types of salad from the salad bar—there was coleslaw; potato salad; raisin; green salad; tomato salad; beetroot salad and bean salad; all with Thousand-Island Dressing; then there was cheesecake; and cheese-and-biscuits—three different kinds of cheese; coffee with cream, in a goblet; brandy; bottles of wine; not to mention the aperitifs to kick off with.

Frankie Well, it's all-in, isn't it?

Vernon It's not, as it happens—that's why I had the lamb-chops.

Jackie No, Mohammed was just saying, you know, he's going to take me out for a nice meal next week. We're gonna go to the Empress Club in Mayfair.

Frankie Oh, that'll be nice for you.

Jackie Yeh, it's a nice club, you know—it's really smart.

Vernon You'll enjoy that, won't you? Right up your street.

Muhammad Excuse?

Vernon (*making a drinking gesture*) Have a little drinkie? Oh, lovely!

Muhammad OK, I take orange juice.

Jackie Orange juice?

Vernon You take orange juice? I'll get you an orange juice.

Irving I hope my wife's watching what she's drinking—I want to get home in one piece!

Jackie That's right, yeh.

Frankie I know how much I can take.

Irving You're mixing them, aren't you? You've been on wine all evening.

Frankie Look, you worry about yourself, and I'll worry about myself, all right?

Irving Well, who's driving, then, you or me?

Frankie I don't mind—you can if you want to.

Irving Well, it's your car—you drive, right?

Frankie All right, all right—don't go on about it.

Irving Right.

Vernon (*pouring orange juice*) Does he want whisky in it? Do you want whisky in it, Abdullah? (*He adds whisky*)

Jackie D'you want whisky, yeh? In your orange juice?

Muhammad Orange juice.

Jackie Yeh, yeh. All right. It's Mohammed, actually.

Vernon Here you are, Smiler.

Muhammad Shukran. [Thank you.]

Frankie Oh.

Vernon Shookra? Is that what it is, Shookra? I like a drop of Shookra.

Jackie Is that what you call it, yah?

Muhammad OK . . . (*He takes out his wad of money*)

Frankie ⎱ ⎧ Oh, Christ . . .
Jackie ⎬ (*together*) ⎨ It's all right, you don't have to pay for it.
Irving ⎰ ⎩ Here, look at that.

Vernon Got a few bob on him, hasn't he?

Jackie Yeh, 'e 'as, you know? (*To Muhammad*) You keep.

Frankie It's free. *Free.*

Vernon Does he want to pay me for it, does he?

Jackie No, don't be stupid.

Muhammad OK, OK, make tip for barman.

Vernon Does he think I'm the barman, does he, eh? I'm not proud, I'll take it—come on, come on.

Irving I should. Have it. Go on! He's got plenty to spare.

Jackie Stop it, yeh? It's probably what they do in his country. What sort of car 'ave you got?

Irving She's got a Clubman.

Frankie Well, we've both got cars, haven't we?

Irving We run two cars!

Frankie Oh yes!

Jackie Mohammed's got a Rolls-Royce.

Irving Oh yes?

Frankie Oh. Rolls-Royce?

Muhammad Rolls-Royce. Many, many.

Jackie Yeh, 'e's got a lot of cars, you know?

Frankie Has he?

Muhammad In my country. (*He empties his glass, and holds it up*)

Vernon Oh—here we go again! (*Taking the glass*) Yes, sir, coming up, sir, at your service, sir. (*He goes to the bar and pours Muhammad another drink*)

Jackie He's got a Cadillac an' all, actually.

Frankie Has he?

Jackie Yeh.

Muhammad English cars no good.

Irving What are you talking about? British cars are the best in the world, Rolls-Royce.

Jackie Well, 'e's got a Rolls, en' 'e?

Irving There you are.

Jackie No, they buy American cars, you know?

Irving Load of tin, they are.
Jackie They're nice and big though, aren't they?
Irving Too big.
Frankie No good in London.
Jackie Yes, but they like limousines, you know—plenty of room in the back.
Irving Put all their wives in, I should think, eh?

Vernon approaches Muhammad with a tea-towel over one arm, and holding Muhammad's drink in the other hand

Vernon Here, Irv, Irv! (*To Muhammad, servile mock-waiter*) Here you are, sir, your drink, sir, at your service, sir.

Vernon and Irving laugh uproariously

Muhammad (*taking the drink, oblivious to the joke*) Elwāhid [Person] go buy Rolls-Royce shop . . .
Jackie Buying a Rolls-Royce yeh?
Muhammad Family go . . . t'gool, [you say,] "OK, take one, two, three." Y'gool, [He says] "La. [No.] No now, soon. Bukra inshallah. [Tomorrow, Allah willing.]" Elwāhid [Person] go, buy American car, is OK, t'gool, [you say,] "OK, take car?" Y'gool, [he says,] "OK, take car halheen, [right now,] take car, shop, go."
Jackie Yeh . . . you take it with you, yeh?
Frankie Oh—cash-and-carry?
Jackie It's fair enough, you know? I mean, if they're paying the money, you've got to come up with the goods.
Irving It's all right if you want a can of beans, isn't it? Some production-line job. But a Rolls-Royce is craftsman-built.
Jackie But you shouldn't 'ave to wait for it.
Irving Course you should.
Jackie No, not for that sort of money.
Irving You don't know what you're talking about.
Jackie It's bad sellin'.
Frankie It's the same with clothes, Ir: you can't keep people hanging around till they're out of fashion.
Jackie That's right.
Irving But you don't get a decent suit off the peg, do you?
Frankie Eh?
Irving You're a fine one to talk, anyway.
Frankie What you talking about?
Irving Your clothes fall apart after five minutes.
Frankie Don't be so bloody stupid.
Irving You're always taking them back.
Jackie It's bad business, I mean, you've got to fulfil your client's demands.
Frankie That's right.
Irving That's all right if you want rubbish. If you want quality, you've got to be prepared to wait.
Vernon If the client says he wants solid-gold door-handles with "Abdullah"

inscribed all over them, he's going to have to wait a couple of weeks for them to turn up, right?

Irving Right.

Jackie 'E's not called Abdullah, actually.

Muhammad Abdullah come here?

Jackie No, 'e's not comin' 'ere.

Pause

Frankie (*to Muhammad*) What exactly do you do, then?

Muhammad (*to Jackie*) Excuse?

Jackie He's a business man.

Frankie Oh, yes?

Jackie (*to Muhammad*) You're in business.

Muhammad (*to Frankie*) Business, business.

Jackie Yeh, he's in oil, you know, Ver.

Vernon Yeh.

Muhammad Er, business, London.

Irving Oh, buying up London, is he, eh?

Jackie Yeh, that's right.

Muhammad holds up his empty glass again

Frankie Oh!

Irving Come on! Chop-chop!

Jackie (*getting up*) It's all right, I'll get it.

Irving (*to Vernon*) Do your job, eh?

Muhammad (*to Jackie*) Is OK: barman make——

Jackie (*taking the glass*) No, no, it's all right, I'll get it.

Vernon He does! He does! He thinks I'm the sodding barman, Jackie!

Jackie No, 'e doesn't, Ver, it's just that I told him that's what this was called, the bar, yeh?

Irving (*following her to the bar*) You know where it is, the orange, do you? Underneath. All right?

Jackie Yeh, I know.

Vernon What're you doing, Irving? Course she knows where it is—she lives here, for Christ's sake. Get out!

Irving All right.

Frankie (*to Muhammad*) Where are you staying?

Muhammad Excuse?

Frankie Oh dear . . .

Vernon Does this character think he's staying here tonight, or what, Jackie?

Jackie Oh no. No, he's just come back for a few drinks, you know? Just wanted to meet some English people, an' that.

Vernon Just so long as we know, right?

Frankie Where . . . are *you* . . . stay-ing . . . ?

Muhammad OK?

Frankie Eh?

Muhammad OK.

Muhammad takes Frankie's wrist and attempts to leave with her. She offers little resistance

Frankie (*remotely enthusiastically*) Oh!

Irving ⎫

Vernon ⎬ (*together*) ⎧ Here! What are you doing?

Jackie ⎭   ⎨ What's he up to?

                      ⎩ What's the matter?

Irving Here! Here, get your mitts off, right?

Muhammad (*to Irving*) Excuse?

Frankie It's all right, Irving, it's all right!

Irving She's mine, right? Mine.

Muhammad Ismāh-ly. [Forgive me.] (*He sits down*)

Irving OK?

Muhammad OK. (*To Jackie*) Make, er . . .

Jackie Yeh, it's all right, don't worry.

Muhammad gestures to Jackie to sit back with him. She does

Yeh—don't worry.

Frankie Where's he staying?

Jackie He's at the *Royal Garden Hotel* in Kensington, actually.

Vernon Probably owns it, doesn't he?

Jackie Yeh, that's right.

Irving In oil, then, is he, eh?

Jackie Yeh, 'e is.

Irving Yeh—like a sardine, eh? (*He laughs uproariously*)

Vernon They own the *Dorchester*, don't they?

Jackie Yeh, they do. (*To Muhammad*) D'you know the *Dorchester*? D'you know, the *Dorchester*?

Muhammad (*to Frankie*) Excuse?

Frankie *DORCHESTER.* No, he doesn't, no.

Irving How many oil-wells you got, then, eh? Oil-wells?

Muhammad Excuse?

Jackie 'T's your business.

Muhammad Business, business.

Jackie Oil.

Irving Oil-wells?

Jackie Yeh, it's his business, you know?

Muhammad Important.

Jackie Yeh . . . oil.

Irving Oil.

Frankie Oh, dear. Look, in the car . . .

Muhammad Car. Many, many.

Frankie Petrol?

Muhammad Petrol.

Frankie Is *oil*.

Muhammad Oyel! OK!

Frankie You see—he understands if you're clear.

Muhammad Means, zēt. [oil.]

Frankie Oh.

Jackie It's your family's business?

Muhammad In my country, is important; very, very.

Irving Yeh, you don't have to tell us.

Jackie Very profitable.

Vernon You're not bloody kidding.

Jackie Very much big money.

Vernon Costs a bloody fortune, doesn't it?

Muhammad Filhasa. Yamm Dhahrān . . . oil . . . ābar azzēt . . .[5] (*He makes a romantic gesture to evoke expansive oil-fields with awe-inspiring monolithic oil-wells here and there*) Ooooh!

Frankie Oh, I say!

Jackie It's your family business?

Irving OPEC?

Muhammad OPEC, na'am. [Yes.] Sheikh Yamani . . .

Irving Sheikh Yam—Shake your money, shake your money, eh? Eh?

Vernon and Irving laugh uproariously

Frankie Don't be so stupid, Irving.

Muhammad You know Sheikh Yamani?

Irving I don't know him, no.

Jackie No, 'e don't know 'im, listen; 't's your family business?

Muhammad Business, business.

Jackie In your country——

Muhammad Big business.

Jackie —your family's business . . .

Muhammad Family.

Jackie At home.

Muhammad Family.

Jackie Where you live.

Muhammad Family.

Jackie Business.

Muhammad Family business.

Jackie Yeh?

Muhammad Is sheep. (*His pronunciation is such that nobody gets it; indeed, it sounds distinctly like "ship"*)

Frankie Eh?

Jackie Ship?

Muhammad Sheep.

Frankie } (*together*) { Oh—ships!
Irving } { Ships.

Jackie Yeh, 'e's in shipping, you know; is it oil-tankers, yeh? Yeh, it's oil-tankers.

Muhammad Import sheep.

Jackie Important, yeh, it's very important, yeh, a lot of big deals go on with that.

Irving Onassis we got here, then, have we?

---

[5] In the Eastern Province. Round Dhahran . . . oil . . . the oilfields.

Jackie 'T's right, yeh.

Vernon He's a magnate.

Muhammad Import sheep, import camel. (*He pronounces the "c" in camel as in "loch"*)

Jackie 'T's imports, yeh?

Muhammad Import sheep.

Frankie Oh, he imports ships.

Jackie Yeh, he buys oil-tankers, you know an' that, Ver?

Muhammad Import sheep, import camel . . .

Irving Import camels?

Jackie No, he doesn't.

Irving That's what he said.

Jackie No, he didn't say that.

Irving He did.

Jackie It must mean something else, yeh? Look: what, do you, import?

Muhammad Camel.

Frankie Oh.

Irving There you are, you see, eh?

Vernon He's a camel importer!

Irving They must be running out!

Vernon and Irving laugh uproariously

Jackie Don't be stupid. (*To Muhammad*) Listen—listen; it's buying and selling?

Muhammad Buy, sell, camel. Many, many camel. He come, Australia.

Frankie Eh?

Vernon He imports camels from Australia!

Frankie No, it's kangaroos!

Jackie No, it must mean something else in his language—look: you do business in Australia?

Muhammad Business, business.

Jackie Yeh. Yeh, he does deals over there.

Muhammad Import sheep, import camel——

Irving There you are!

Muhammad —import, em . . .

Jackie Is it oil?

Muhammad Is, eh . . .

Jackie You buy oil? Yeh, 'e buys oil, yeh. Is it oil-tankers? Yeh, it's oil-tankers.

Muhammad Er . . . sakhla . . . [goat . . .] (*He gestures vaguely*)

Frankie No . . .

Muhammad Is . . .

Frankie He's trying to say something.

Muhammad Make, er . . . (*He mimes vaguely*)

Frankie Moving?

Jackie No, it's not moving, no.

Muhammad Make, er . . .

Jackie Is ships, yeh? Big ships on the sea? Yeh, they are big, you know?

Muhammad Sheep, big . . . sheep.
Irving Boxes?
Jackie No, it's not boxes.
Irving Crates?
Jackie Crates, yeh. You put stuff in crates?
Vernon Bloody cargo, isn't it?
Irving Course it is.
Jackie Is it cargo—you know, ship's cargo?
Muhammad Sheep.
Jackie What sort of cargo is it?
Muhammad Sheep ma'a, [with,] mm . . . (*He mimes two horns*)
Frankie Oh, hats, is it? Hats?
Jackie No, no, it's not hats.
Muhammad Er, sheep ma'a—"Baa!" (*He mimes a goat ramming a wall, one hand as the goat, the other as the wall*)
Frankie Oh, Christ!
Jackie No, don't understand.
Muhammad Is er, sheep, ma'a . . . (*He mimes milking udders*)
Irving Here—is it a book or a film?
Frankie Please, Irving!

Vernon and Irving laugh uproariously

Muhammad Make, er . . . (*He picks up the rug and uses it as a moving creature*)
Jackie No, it's fur, yeh, he's in the fur trade.
Frankie Oh, wildlife, is it?
Vernon Here—don't do that with the bloody rug!
Jackie No, it's all right, Ver, 'e's just trying to explain.
Vernon He doesn't have to rip the place apart, does he? God almighty.
Jackie No, well 'e wasn't; 'e was just showing you.

Frankie helps Vernon to put the rug back; this develops into a brief surreptitious fondling session, which nobody else notices

Frankie (*to Muhammad*) Mind your feet.
Jackie You're in the fur trade?
Muhammad Goat. (*His pronunciation is such that they still don't get it*)
Jackie Good.
Frankie (*moving Muhammad's feet*) Good? Oh, he likes this.
Muhammad Is goat.
Jackie Is good? Is good fur, yeh?
Muhammad (*holding up his empty glass*) Where barman?
Jackie 'S the matter, d'you want another drink?
Muhammad (*to Vernon*) Ya—khooyi. [Hey—my friend.]
Jackie (*taking the glass*) No, it's all right, I'll get it for you. (*She goes to the bar and pours another drink for Muhammad*)
Muhammad Er, goat.
Jackie Yeh, good, yeh, good trade, you know? It's worth spending a few

grand on a really good fur coat, you know, it's an investment, init, there's always goin' to be a demand for that sort of thing . . .

Irving That's right.

Jackie It's like gold an' jewellery an' that, specially at the moment . . .

Irving Yeh.

Jackie My dad got me my jacket you know for my twenty-first I mean it's only imitation oh no no it's genuine fox you know but I mean 'e said if I go to interviews an' that I'm goin' to look a bit special you know a cut above the rest.

Irving Well, you want to make an impression.

Jackie That's right, yeh. Shows you've got the money to spend you know and money talks.

Irving Yeh.

Jackie My mum always 'ad a fur coat she 'ad this lovely astrakhan, my mum's funeral my auntie come down from Birmingham she 'ad this lovely short fur grey jacket on you know it looked really special really glamorous.

Irving Chic, isn't it?

Jackie It was a really foggy day.

Irving I've got a sheepskin rally coat.

Jackie Oh yeh well a lot of business men wear them you know yeh.

Irving Wrap it round you, pull the collar up, surprising.

Jackie Yeh, well you get these weirdos on telly an' that saying they shouldn't kill the animals but I mean let's face it it's only the very rich person that can afford a good mink you know so they can't kill that many animals, can they?

Irving Right.

Muhammad Goat.

Jackie (*giving Muhammad his drink*) Good? Yeh, it's a good trade.

Muhammad Import goat.

Jackie Imports and exports, yeh, it's very good.

Muhammad Import goat, import camel.

Irving Import camel!

Jackie No, look, it's camel coats, yeh?

Muhammad Import sheep.

Jackie Yeh . . .

Frankie Import ships, yes we got that.

Muhammad Import sheep, import camel.

Vernon Import ship, import camel!

Muhammad Is sheep, is camel, is goat.

Vernon Is sheep, is camel, is *goat*!

Vernon and Irving laugh uproariously

Irving Goat, eh?

Jackie No—it isn't!

Irving Well—goatskins, eh?

Jackie No, it's not!!

Irving Goat, is it? Eh? (*He mimes goat horns and makes goat noises*) Eh?

(*He laughs uproariously*)

Muhammad Goat. Er . . . is goat! GOAT!! (*He repeats his own goat mime and noises of earlier*)

Frankie		⌈Christ, it is goat!
Irving	(*together*)	⟨Goat!
Vernon		It is goat!
Jackie		⌊No!!!

Muhammad Is sheep. Sheep, meehh! Sheep, sheep, meeehh!

Frankie		
Irving	(*together*)	⟨Sheep!
Vernon		
Jackie No!		

Muhammad		
Frankie	(*together*)	⟨Is sheep, is camel, is goat!
Irving		
Vernon		
Jackie No, it isn't!!		

Vernon and Irving are helpless with laughter and glee

Vernon I don't believe it—he's a bloody sheep farmer!

Jackie No, no, 'e's not! 'E's just got 'is animals mixed up. (*She throws herself on the floor and demonstrates with the rug*) Look—it's mink, yeh? Leopard skin?

Frankie No, it isn't, Jackie.

Jackie It is.

Frankie It isn't—he imports sheep and camels and goats, he just said so.

Jackie Yes, but 'e don't know the words in English.

Frankie He doesn't speak English.

Jackie (*to Muhammad*) Look? 'T's animals, yeh? It's fur?

Muhammad For. (*His pronunciation sounds like "fur"*)

Jackie What sort of animal is it?

Muhammad For Hajj.[6]

Jackie No, 'e don't understand. (*She gets up and moves away*)

Frankie Fur hedge, is it? Oi! A fur hedge?

Muhammad Hajj.

Frankie Hedge?

Muhammad Na'am, [Yes,] Hajj. For Hajj.

Frankie Oh, hats? Fur hats?

Jackie No!

Frankie You see, I said it was hats.

Irving No, they don't have fur hats in Arabia, do they?

Jackie No, that's right, they don't, no.

Muhammad For Hajj.

Irving Fur-hudge? Fudge? No, Turkish Delight, you have, eh?

Vernon and Irving laugh uproariously

---

[6] The Hajj is the Great Pilgrimage to Mecca. Every Muslim is expected to undertake the Hajj at least once in his life.

Muhammad Hajj, Hajj!!
Vernon Hedgehogs! Hedgehogs! He imports hedgehogs!
Jackie It's not funny, Ver—just leave 'im alone, will you?
Muhammad Is OK. Hadhoula Kuffar. Make er—mm—addeen. Is OK.
Ashrah-lahum, er ... I speak him; Allāhu 'aleemum bimā fi guloob innās.[7]
Vernon Allahoo li-oggly oggly-wiggly!
Irving Yeh, we had one at home, the knob dropped off, eh?

Vernon and Irving laugh uproariously

Muhammad Er, Hajj, er go, er Mecca.
Frankie Mocca?
Muhammad Go. Mecca.
Frankie Oh, Mocha coffee is it?
Muhammad Coffee?
Frankie Mm.
Muhammad Coffee-pot. Import coffee-pot.
Frankie Oh, he imports coffee-pots.
Jackie No ...
Muhammad In, er, suq [market], in Jiddha, is er, one, two, three coffee-pot, is carpet.
Frankie Soup, coffee-pots, carpets ...
Irving Got a shop, have you? Shop?
Frankie Shop?
Muhammad Shop, shop. Many. OK ... OK ... Hajj. Hajj is important, very, very. Is make, er Islam, make, er, Islam ...
Irving Islam?
Muhammad Make, er, Islam, go Mecca, er, go Mecca ...
Vernon Mecca! He's talking about bloody Mecca!
Frankie Oh, Mecca!
Irving They all go down the **Muhammad** Go Mecca ... Go
Locarno, don't they?   Arafat ... Go Muzdalifah, go
                                         Mina, Mina is Id el Adha.[8]

Irving and Vernon laugh uproariously

Muhammad Excuse ... Mina is sheep——
Frankie ⎫
Vernon ⎬ *(together)*—is camel, is goat.
Irving ⎭
Frankie Yes ...
Muhammad OK, Mina is sheep——
Irving ⎫
Vernon ⎪
Frankie ⎬ *(together)*—is camel, is goat ...
Muhammad ⎭

---

[7] Is OK. They are unbelievers. Make er—mm—our religion. Is OK. I will
explain to them, er... I speak him; Allah is aware what is in people's hearts.

[8] Mina is the Feast of the Sacrifice.

Irving Yes?
Muhammad Make, go ... (*He makes a throat-slitting gesture*)
Frankie Oh! Chop their heads off?
Vernon Oh, do you?
Irving Slit their throats, eh? You got an abattoir?
Muhammad For Allah.
Vernon For Allah?
Muhammad For Allah.

Jackie sits at the dining-table, alone. She is very upset

Vernon Sheep and camel and your goats, you slit their throats for Allah—
   Oh, I see, you take them to Mecca ...
Irving Oh, I see ...
Vernon Your sheep and camels and goats, you go to Mecca and sacrifice
   'em for Allah! Very nice!
Muhammad So is sheep——
Vernon
Irving
Frankie } (*together*)—is camel, is goat——
Muhammad
Muhammad —is suq in Jiddha, is coffee-pot, is carpet ...
Irving For tourists, is it?
Muhammad Is family business.
Frankie You see, he's got a shop, Jackie.

Pause

Muhammad Wa [And] umbrella.
Frankie Eh?
Muhammad Umbrella.
Frankie Umbrella?
Irving Rain a lot, does it?
Muhammad Is hot, like this like this like this, make Marwan come
   London, buy umbrella.
Irving Well, you've come to the right place, then.
Muhammad Important ...
Irving London ...
Muhammad London ...
Irving Best umbrellas in the world, you know.
Muhammad Umbrella. (*He holds up his empty glass*)
Frankie (*taking his glass*) Oh, he wants another one.
Vernon Same again, Sabu?

Pause

Irving (*to Jackie*) Takes all sorts, eh? (*He laughs uproariously*)
Muhammad (*to Jackie*) OK?

No reaction from Jackie. Pause

Frankie What's the matter with you?
Irving Eh?

Muhammad (*to Jackie*) OK, I come now?

Vernon How about you, Jackie? Drink?

Jackie No, I'm all right.

Vernon Want a whisky?

Jackie No. Just going to powder me nose, actually.

Jackie exits to her room, hastily. A door closes, off

Irving follows Jackie

Muhammad (*getting up*) I come now?

Vernon (*giving Muhammad his glass*) Here you are, Gungha Din—get that down you.

The door opens, off

Irving (*off*) D'you want a whisky?

Jackie (*off*) No, I'm just putting some lipstick on, yeh?

The door closes, off, then opens again

Irving (*off*) What's the matter? Are you all right?

Jackie (*off*) Get out of my room, yeh?

The door slams violently, off. Pause

Irving enters

Vernon What are you up to, Irving?

Irving Nothing. What d'you mean?

Muhammad holds up his empty glass

Frankie (*taking the glass*) Finished, have you?

Muhammad goes into the hall

Muhammad (*as he goes*) Where he go?

Muhammad exits towards Jackie's room

Irving (*following him into the hall*) Here, where are you going?

Muhammad knocks on Jackie's door, off

You can't go in there.

The door opens, off

Jackie (*off*) Stop following me about!!

Muhammad staggers backwards into view as Jackie pushes him hard

Irving All right? Got the message?

The door closes, off

Vernon Irving!

Irving Look, it's not me! Now you keep out of there, right?

Vernon What's going on? Are you all right, Jackie?

Irving Yeh, she's all right.

Jackie (*off*) I'm just trying to put me lipstick on, y'know?

Vernon Come in here, the pair of you, you're as bad as each other. God almighty! Children!

Muhammad (*muttering*) Wallah ... [By Allah ...] (*He closes the lounge door from the hall*)

Irving Hey! (*He opens the door, and goes into the hall*)

Muhammad disappears towards Jackie's room, followed by Irving

(*Off*) Hey, Sambo: what're you standing there for, eh?

Frankie closes the door

Frankie Come on then: who is she?	**Muhammad** (*off*) Excuse?
Vernon Who?	**Irving** (*off; quietly*) You're not
Frankie Maggie.	going in there, you know.
Vernon Maggie?	**Muhammad** (*off; quietly*) Excuse?
Frankie Yes—Maggie.	**Irving** (*off; quietly*) You just keep
	out, right?

Vernon Maggie is an old friend of mine. She's separated from her husband, she's got a little kiddy called Wayne, who wears glasses, and happens to have a hole in his heart, and sometimes I take them out, for his benefit, right? Last weekend we went to the zoo. And there's nothing going on between me and Maggie.

Frankie Well, that's not what I heard from Irving.

Vernon Oh, Irving's got a very vivid imagination, hasn't he? I've only got to mention a girl's name, and he invents a whole bloody romance for me.

Frankie But you could've phoned me, Ver; it's been three weeks.

Vernon I told you, Frankie: I wanted to let the dust settle; right?

Muhammad (*off*) What her name?

Irving (*off*) Jackie.

Muhammad (*off*) Excuse?

Irving (*off*) Jackie.

Muhammad (*off*) Ja ... r ... k ...

Irving (*off*) That's her room, and you're not going in there.

Muhammad (*off*) Jah ...

Frankie Well, I don't know what to think. I really don't.

Vernon embraces her from behind

Vernon You do believe me, don't you, Frankie? I wouldn't lie to you, you know that, don't you? Trust me, Frankie. You do trust me, don't you?

Frankie (*turning to him*) Of course I trust you, Vernon.

They kiss, standing behind the sofa

Muhammad knocks on Jackie's door, off

Irving (*off, to Muhammad*) What're you doing?

The door opens, off

Jackie (*off*) Leave me alone, will you? It's my room, you know?

Irving (*off*) I've been trying to keep him out of there.

Jackie, Irving and Muhammad enter

Vernon immediately terminates the embrace by dropping Frankie backwards over the sofa

Vernon For Christ's sake, Frankie! Mind the bloody sofa!
Irving What're you doing?
Vernon She's sitting on the back of the sofa, and goes arse over tip.

Frankie rushes out to the kitchen

God almighty! I wouldn't let her drive you home, Irving.
Irving What d'you mean?
Vernon She's had too much. She's drunk.
Irving (*going towards the door*) Get out of the way, Sambo.
Muhammad OK, make——
Irving All right!! All right!!

Irving exits

Muhammad closes the door behind Irving

Vernon (*tidying up*) Look at the state of this—treating the place like a gymnasium, she's out of control.
Jackie What's the matter with her, Ver?
Vernon She can't take her drink, Jackie. She's an alcoholic.
Jackie Oh, really?
Vernon Mm.
Jackie Thought it was a bit funny you know when I come in; I wondered what was goin' on. (*She sits down*)

Irving and Frankie can be heard having a subdued row, off, in the kitchen

Muhammad Is OK, I make him . . . er . . .
Jackie What's the matter?
Muhammad Excuse?
Jackie Just 'avin' a whisky—all right?
Muhammad La! [No!]

Irving enters

Irving Well, I'm not driving.

He goes straight out again

Muhammad Orange juice.
Vernon You getting any bother, Jackie?
Jackie No, it's all right.
Muhammad OK: Barman—orange juice.
Vernon Tell him I'm not the sodding barman, Jackie!
Jackie No, it's all right, he knows that, Vernon—just go and sit down, yeh? Go and sit down!
Muhammad OK. (*He gets hold of Jackie's arm*)
Jackie Don't pull me!
Vernon Hey!

Jackie 'T's all right, Ver, I can handle it.
Muhammad (*patting the sofa*) OK, make ...
Jackie Don't pat the seat, I'm not a servant.
Muhammad Make, er, make ...

Irving enters

Vernon D'you want a brandy, Irv?
Irving Yes, please. In there.
Vernon She's had too much, Irving.
Irving You don't have to tell me.

Muhammad gets up

She's not having any more, right?
Vernon It's not up to me, Irving.   *Muhammad makes some attempt to*
Irving Yeh, well don't you give her   *get Jackie up*
any.
                                          Jackie 'T's the matter?
Vernon She's your wife, Irving,   **Muhammad** OK ...
she's your responsibility. You   **Jackie** Just go and sit down, yeh?
keep an eye on her. Right.   Get off me!
                                          Muhammad Is OK ...
                                          Jackie Just get off me, yeh?!!

Irving Oi! You keep your hands to yourself!
Muhammad Wallah ... [By Allah ...]
Vernon Come on, come on! Sit yourself down, have a little relax, and I'll
get you an orange juice.
Muhammad (*sitting down*) Hadha kelb! [He is a dog!]
Vernon (*pouring Muhammad a drink*) Oh, you don't have to tell me—I
have to work with him!
Irving You taking his side now, are you? You want to learn some manners
before you come over here.
Muhammad Ēsh hal warta! [What a situation!]
Irving You all right?
Jackie Yeh. It's my stockings.
Irving Sure? (*Nearly touching her legs*) Not bruised, are you?
Jackie No, it's all right!
Muhammad (*muttering*) Hadhy haggety, hadheech haggety, killihin
haggāty ...[9]
Irving Diabolical liberty!
Vernon (*giving Muhammad his drink*) Here you are.
Muhammad Minhu hādha? [Who is this person?]
Vernon I know!!
Irving What are you driving at the moment?
Jackie Well, I haven't actually got a car at the moment.
Irving Haven't you?
Jackie No, well I can't really afford—well, I can afford it, we get taxis laid
on at work an' that, you know, it's a perk of the job.

---

[9] This one's mine, that one's mine, all of them are mine ...

Irving Nice to have your own wheels isn't it, though, be independent?

Jackie Yeh. Well, I'll probably get one later on.

Irving You don't want to go phoning taxis during the day, waiting for them to turn up.

Jackie Don't need one during the day. I work at night. I sleep during the day.

Irving Do you?

Jackie I'm more of a night person anyway, actually.

Irving What sort of car d'you fancy then, eh?

Jackie Dunno . . . I might get a sports-car . . .

Irving Yeh, I can just see you in a nice MGB, you know.

Jackie Oh, yeh, they're nice-looking cars.

Irving They are, yes; still, if you want one, you're going to have to move fast, 'cos they're going to be collectors' items soon.

Vernon You trying to sell to Jackie, Irving? Moving in on my territory?

Irving First come, first served!

Vernon No, you go ahead. I make it a rule, never to sell to friends.

Jackie No, that's right, actually, Vern.

Irving I'll do anyone a favour.

Vernon No, no, if you sell to a friend, there's a fault in the product, they come back, complain, ends up on your bloody doorstep, that way you destroy a perfectly good relationship.

Jackie Yeh . . .

Irving No problem—I keep business quite separate.

Jackie No, you can't you know . . . I've worked in selling, yeh, an' it don't pay to get involved in your prospects. 'T's bad business.

Vernon Yeh.

Irving You can't say we're exactly involved, you and me, can you, eh?

Jackie I'm not saying that.

Irving Not yet, anyway. Eh? Chance'd be a fine thing, eh? (*He laughs uproariously*)

Muhammad lights a cigarette, and throws his match on the floor

Here, what're you doing?

Vernon Hi, not on the carpet, you bloody cretin!

Irving You're not in the desert now, you know?

Vernon Matches go in the ashtray—Ancient English Custom—compris?

Irving Go on, get back to your tent!

Frankie enters eating a piece of melon and a buttered roll

Frankie What're you going on about now, Irving?

Irving What's the matter with you, then?

Frankie There's nothing the matter with me—you're the one with the big mouth!

Irving You fat Arab!

Frankie Oh, for Christ's sake, Irving!

Irving You drunken slut!

Frankie You what?

Irving Mind where you're walking!

Frankie Oh, shut up!

Irving Don't trip over the rug!

Frankie I'm not listening, Irving! (*She sits next to Muhammad on the sofa*)

Irving Here, watch it—you'll fall off the edge if you're not careful!

Frankie It's going straight in one ear, and out the other, all right?

Irving Just watch it, right?

Vernon exits to the kitchen

Muhammad Hadha kelb. [He is a dog.]

Frankie Eh?

Muhammad Ey-wa, kelb ibn kelb! [Absolutely—a dog—the son of a dog!]

Frankie Yeh, I know, that's how I feel about him, too.

Irving Why don't you blow in his ear?

Frankie Oh, shut up, Irving!!

Vernon enters with a dustpan, into which he empties the ashtrays

Vernon Christ almighty, Frankie; are you eating again?

Frankie Yes, I am, Vernon, if it's all the same to you.

Irving She's got worms.

Frankie Sod off, Irving!

Vernon You've just had a five-course meal, for Christ's sake! Cost me forty-nine quid!

Jackie Oh, really? 'T's a lot of money, you know?

Vernon exits to the kitchen, followed by Irving

Irving (*off*) Hullo, Mrs Mop's on the job, then, eh?

Frankie (*to Muhammad*) Are you all right?

Jackie Yeh, 'e's all right.

Frankie I wasn't asking you.

Pause

Irving enters

Jackie No, I was just telling you. (*To Irving*) What sort of car have you got at the moment?

Irving Metro HLE.

Jackie Oh, really? How long 'ave you 'ad it?

Irving Couple of months.

Vernon enters

Jackie Oh, yeh? How's it goin'?

Irving Oh, really well.

Jackie Yeh?

Irving Lot of Driver-Satisfaction.

Jackie Oh yeh? Not had any trouble with it?

Irving No—no; no, no.

Vernon What d'you mean, no?

Irving Well, it's only the carburettor, you know, fifteen-minute job.
Frankie Drives it too bloody fast, that's why.
Irving Chance'd be a fine thing—the North Circular's always jam-packed.
Jackie 'T's bad, though, if you've only had it a few months.
Vernon No, no, Jackie—it's a first-rate motor.
Jackie Yeh, but you want reliability, don't you?
Vernon No, all the road reports in the trade press are agreed: Car of the Decade.
Irving Without a doubt, it's the most economical car on the road in Europe today.
Vernon Engineering-wise, it's a breakthrough.
Irving With the split-action rear seat, you've got really versatile loadability.
Vernon You've got Small Car Manoeuvrability, Big Car Comfort.
Jackie It's nicely finished.
Irving Superbly so, yes.
Jackie You can't get them, can you? You've got to wait about six months or something.
Irving No, well, that's all down to the Unions, isn't it?
Jackie 'T's right.
Vernon We've just been feeling the shock-waves of industrial action; that's all cleared up now.
Jackie 'T's disgusting, you know. That's the trouble with this country.
Irving It's the Communists, you see.
Jackie 'T's right, yeh.
Irving They're behind the Unions.
Jackie Yeh, yeh.
Irving If we got rid of the Communists, we'd all be much better off.
Frankie Bloody Communists!
Muhammad Kumnis?
Frankie Eh?
Muhammad Him?
Frankie No, he's not a Communist, no!
Irving No!
Jackie No ... we get a lot of Communists in this country.
Muhammad No good!
Jackie No, that's right.
Muhammad In my country, no kumnis.
Jackie They don't have 'em, you know.
Muhammad Wallah. Hādhōla fitna. In many country is—Ghadafi fi Leebya, suf al Yemen wal 'Arāq u Eerān. Wallah. Ash-Shāh al-meskeen. Ash Shāh——[10]
Vernon The Shah, yeh.
Muhammad Hādhōla ashee'ay. Those Shi-ites. Wallah. Ash-Shāh. (*He makes a throat-slitting gesture*)
Irving Yes, slit their throats—best thing for 'em.

---

[10] By Allah. They are a nuisance. In many country is—Ghadafi of Libya, look at Yemen and Iraq and Iran. By Allah. The Shah, the poor Shah—

Frankie Quite right.

Jackie That's why it's a rich country, you know. It's like my job, there's no union in that, 't's much better.

Irving Really?

Jackie Anyone starts any trouble, that's it, they're out.

Irving That's right.

Vernon Same with your job, isn't it, Frankie?

Frankie Eh?

Vernon No unions in your job, are there?

Jackie What d'you do?

Irving Sits on her backside all day.

Frankie That's not true, Ir.

Irving No?

Frankie I'm in-between jobs at the moment.

Vernon You have been for the last five years, haven't you, Frankie?

Irving Seven years, actually.

Frankie Six, if you must know.

Jackie That's why British firms've got a bad reputation. I mean, you don't drive a Metro, do you, Ver?

Irving $\left.\right\}$ (*together*) $\left\{\right.$ He's got an Ital.

Vernon I've got an Ital.

Jackie That's right, yeh.

Vernon British car.

Jackie Oh?—Yeh, I know.

Vernon More power than Metro—more oomph.

Irving Just that bit more poke, eh? (*He laughs uproariously*)

Frankie Please.

Irving More difficult to park, though, isn't it?

Vernon I don't have any trouble parking, Irving.

Irving No, nor do I—I'll fit into any space, eh? The tighter the better! (*He now has a spasm of uproarious laughter quite unprecedented in its length and its uncontrolled hysteria, not to mention its obscenity. A short pause, then . . .*) Oops!—Excuse me!

Irving exits hurriedly to the toilet

Pause. Muhammad holds up his empty glass

Vernon Oh, here we go again—more shookra. (*He takes the glass and goes to the bar*)

Muhammad Where . . . al kumnis?

Frankie No, he's not a Communist, no!

Muhammad No good!

Pause. Vernon brings Muhammad his drink

Vernon Here y'are, Genghis. (*He tousles Muhammad's hair*) All right?

Frankie D'you want some more melon?

Jackie No, he's OK.

Frankie I'm just asking him.

Muhammad What your name?
Frankie Frances.
Muhammad Excuse?
Frankie Frankie. Fran—kie.
Muhammad Frarn . . . k.
Frankie That's right.
Muhammad (*indicating*) Is Jar . . . k.
Frankie Mm. Would you like some melon?
Jackie 'E's probably had something to eat in the hotel.
Frankie Well, he might be feeling a bit peckish by now, mightn't he? Melon?
Muhammad Melon. It mean "hub-hub". In my country, is mewa, [sweet,] for eat. Is big. Is good. Hub-hub.
Frankie Well, would you like some?
Jackie He's just tellin' you what it's called, that's all.
Frankie Yes, I know that. (*To Muhammad*) Would you, like, some melon?
Vernon Come on, Frankie—it's only a little bit of green skin—I'm sure you can manage that.
Frankie Honestly, Vernon! (*To Muhammad*) I'll get you some, anyway.

Frankie exits to the kitchen

Muhammad (*following her into the hall*) I come now?
Jackie (*following him to the door*) No, that's all right. What's the matter?
Muhammad (*not having seen where Frankie went*) Where he go?
Jackie Where are you going?

Muhammad wanders down the corridor

Vernon He's going to the toilet. Form a queue!

Frankie enters, with a piece of melon and a spoon on a dish

Frankie Where is he, then?
Vernon He's under the sofa, look—can't you see his little feet?
Frankie Oh, for Christ's sake. (*Going into the hall*) Coo-eee!

Frankie wanders off after Muhammad

Jackie Are you all right, Ver?
Vernon I'm all right, Jackie—how are you?
Jackie I'm all right. I'm a bit tired, actually.
Vernon Yeh?
Jackie 'Ow old is she?
Vernon She's got to be forty.
Jackie Yeh, she looks it, actually. (*Frankie is, of course, much nearer 30 than 40*)
Vernon Mm.
Jackie 'E's a bit loud-mouthed, an' all, isn't 'e?
Vernon You're not bloody kidding. He's like that at work, all day long—rabbit, rabbit.
Jackie Does 'e sell?

Vernon No.

Jackie No, they don't, them blokes; I've seen 'em before, it's all talk no action.

Vernon He'll get the push before the end of the year.

Jackie Oh, really?

Vernon Yup.

Irving (*off, in the loo*) What's going on?

Vernon Want a whisky?

Jackie Yeh, all right.

Irving (*off*) Frankie!

Frankie (*off*) Nothing!

Irving (*off*) What're you doing?

Frankie (*off*) I'm just giving him his melon.

Irving (*off*) Who?

Frankie (*off*) Mo-hammed.

Frankie enters, still with the bowl and melon

Come on; come and have your melon—come on! Come on! Come on!

Muhammad enters, with his jacket mostly off

Jackie What's the matter with him?

Frankie Nothing.

Jackie Come and get your jacket on. Can you hold that, Ver? (*She hands him her glass*) 'T's all right. I'll help you.

Frankie I think he's a bit hot, actually.

Jackie Well, 'e doesn't want it 'anging off 'im, does 'e?

Muhammad Barman, is el kumnis, is, make, er, Fran for him, is Jack for him, kumnis make, er, is, make . . . (*He slaps the sole of his foot with his hand*)

Jackie No, Mohammed, listen to me; listen to me—come and sit down, yeh?

Frankie Come on, come and sit down with your melon. Come on.

Jackie Come and sit over here, yeh?

Frankie No, he's all right here. Come on.

Muhammad sits on the sofa with Frankie

Muhammad (*muttering*) Wallah hādhōla fitna. Fi kill mukān. Suf al Yemen wal 'Arāq u Eerān . . .[11]

Frankie Here you are—melon.

Jackie No, 'e doesn't want that, actually.

Frankie He might.

Jackie Yeh, he might not.

Frankie Melon.

Muhammad What him?

Frankie Melon.

Jackie Can I 'ave my whisky, Ver?

---

[11] By Allah they are a nuisance. Everywhere. Look at Yemen and Iraq and Iran . . .

Muhammad Melon, mean, "hub-hub". In my country—
Vernon Oh, shut up and eat your sodding melon!

Irving enters

Irving Go on—get it down you; don't waste it! It doesn't grow on trees, does it, eh? (*He laughs uproariously*)
Vernon Here, Irving: see if he wants a nut on it.
Irving Eh?
Vernon See if he wants a nut on his melon. (*He passes the nuts to Irving*)
Irving Oh, yeh, look you haven't got any garnish, have you? Here you are.
   (*He sprinkles peanuts on the melon*)

Frankie		For Christ's sake, Irving, he's not a bloody monkey!
Irving	(*together*)	You'll like these, they're your favourites.
Jackie		Oh, no look, leave him alone—you don't have nuts on melon.

Muhammad Wallah ...
Jackie Are you all right?
Muhammad Shukran. [Thank you.]
Jackie What?
Muhammad Shukran.
Jackie Sugar, yeh? D'you want some sugar on it? (*She gets up*)
Vernon Shookra! He wants a drop of shookra!
Irving Give him some shookra on his nuts, eh?
Muhammad (*getting up*) I come now?
Vernon I'll give him a drop of shookra.
Jackie Oh, no, don't be stupid, Ver, don't wind 'im up, you know?
Vernon It's all right, Jackie, I'm only kidding.

Jackie exits to the kitchen

Vernon immediately pours whisky on the melon

Frankie Jesus Christ! What a waste!

Irving laughs uproariously

   Dear, oh dear!
Irving Go on, get it down you!

Jackie enters with the sugar-bowl

Jackie Here y'are, 't's all right, I've got you some. Come and sit down, yeh?
Muhammad (*going towards the door*) OK, Jack, make, er ... (*He gestures to Jackie to go with him*)
Irving Go on! Go on!
Vernon Leave her. Come and eat your melon. Where are you going? Come and eat your nice melon!
Irving Go on! Bye bye! Clear off! Go on! Off you go!
Muhammad Allah ykhalleek.¹² Al kumnis make——

---

¹² Allah preserve you. (May Allah preserve you from my wrath.)

Irving Here. Look. I am not a Communist. Right?

Muhammad Kumnis, kumnis make——

Irving I am not—listen to me, Sambo: I am not a Communist.

Frankie wanders over to the bar and pours herself a drink

Muhammad Kumnis!

Vernon He is! He is! He is a Communist!

Irving ⎫   ⎧I am not a Communist!

Vernon ⎬ *(together)* ⎨He is a Communist!

Muhammad ⎭   ⎩Kumnis!

Vernon Here, Irving! Irving! Look, your wife's having a drink, look!

Irving rushes over to Frankie at the bar. Throughout the next passage Vernon laughs uproariously

Frankie You bloody sneak, Vernon Staines.

Irving confiscates her glass

    Give me my glass back!

Irving You're not having any more, right?

Frankie All right. (*She grabs the whisky bottle*) Then I'll have whisky.

Irving (*taking the bottle*) You will not!

Frankie All right then. (*She grabs the vodka bottle*) Vodka—I like vodka!

Irving (*taking the bottle*) You give me that.

Frankie Give me my glass back, Irving!

Irving No.

Frankie Come on, I'm not going to ask you again—give me my bloody glass back!

Irving You've had enough, right?

Frankie Jesus Christ, Irving: give me my glass!

Irving Just get away!

Frankie No.

Irving Look: you want a drink, get yourself an orange juice.

Frankie I don't want bloody orange juice, I want a gin and tonic, now, come on, give me my glass back!

Irving You're not driving in this state.

Frankie All right, then, we'll get a taxi, OK? Now give me that glass.

Irving Oh, right, yeh, we'll get a taxi, OK—that's why we run two cars, isn't it? So's every time we go out, we get a taxi.

Frankie I'm not going to ask you again!

Irving Right. OK. Drink away, then. Go on. Help yourself.

Frankie Dear, oh dear.

Irving OK, yeh: we'll get a taxi. I'm the one that's going to have to pay for it, aren't I?

Frankie I don't mind—I'll pay for it.

Irving Oh yes—what with?

Frankie With my money, what d'you think?

Irving What money?

Frankie The money I've got in my purse, Irving.
Irving Yeh—where d'you get that from, eh?
Frankie Don't be so bloody mean.
Irving Why don't you try going out to work, eh?
Frankie I don't call poncing around a bloody car showroom all day work, Irving.

Vernon finds this particularly amusing

Irving Right, we're getting rid of your car.
Frankie Bloody Scrooge.
Irving You only use it for going up to the end of the road, to the shops.
Frankie Oh, sod off, Irving!
Jackie Charming!
Irving (*to Muhammad*) What's the matter with you, Sambo, eh? Had your eyeful? Go on, clear off!
Vernon He's all right, Irving.
Muhammad OK, khallās, [it is the end,] Barman—
Vernon Hey: I'm not a barman.
Muhammad Utrud. [Throw him out.] (*He gestures throwing Irving out*) Utrud hadha. [Throw this person out.] (*He makes a similar gesture*) Halheen. [Right now.] OK, I speak . . . this is Jack, girl, mm (*he gestures denoting himself*) this Fran, girl . . . mm (*he makes a similar gesture*) al kumnis—
Irving Hey! Hey! Hey! I am not a Communist, right? I'm a Conservative, and proud of it! And I'll tell you something else for nothing . . . (*Taking Frankie's wrist*) She is mine, right? Mine. My wife. My . . . wife. OK? (*He drops her wrist*)

Pause

Muhammad Wife?
Irving Wife.
Muhammad Fran, wife?
Frankie Yes. Unfortunately.
Muhammad Wallah . . .

Pause

Frankie Are you married, are you?
Jackie No, 'e's not.
Frankie How do you know?
Jackie I know 'is friend, yeh, and 'e isn't.
Frankie Well, let's ask him, shall we? Have you got a wife?
Jackie What's the matter, don't you believe me?
Frankie *You*, got a *wife*?

During the following speech, Muhammad is mocked and mimicked by Irving

Muhammad (*tutting*) Hādha suāl mustaheel. Ana Areby. Mā lāzim tas'al an il-hareem! Mā lāzim tas'al an addeen! Hādha ihāna! Antum wukeheen, antum al Inglees! Ana Araby. OK?[13]

Jackie All right?

Muhammad OK—Barman——

Vernon Hey, let's clear this up, once and for all, you and me, shall we? I'm not a barman. Right? Understand?

Muhammad Orange juice.

Vernon Listen, you ignorant bloody golliwog, what have you got in there, sawdust? I've just told you: I'm not the barman. I live here. This is my flat. This is my chair. My music centre. My television. My bar. My sofa. My lodger. My property. Right. Understand? Has it gone in? Good! Jesus Christ!

Muhammad Barman: taxi!

Vernon (*shouting*) Listen! I'm not a barman! Repeat: not a barman!! You want to know what I do for a living? I'll tell you what I do for a living: I sell motor cars—you know what I mean? Cars? Vroom-vroom? Ey? You want to buy a car, I'll sell you a car, here you are—(*he picks up a brochure*)—Mini: a little car for a little man. Very appropriate! I'm a car salesman, I'm not a barman. (*He bangs Muhammad on the head with the rolled-up brochure*) Boom-boom!!

Muhammad (*moving towards the table*) Jack: make taxi! Jack . . . telefoon taxi!

Jackie Don't hit me.

Irving Keep your hands to yourself.

Muhammad Jack—taxi!

Jackie Get off me, yeh?

Irving (*assaulting Muhammad*) How many more times have you got to be told, eh?!!!

Muhammad *Barman!!*

Vernon (*screaming*) I'm not a barman!! I'm not a barman!! I'm not a barman!! I'm not a barman!! I'm not a barman!! I'm not a barman!! I'm not a barman!! I'm not a barman!! I'm not a sodding barman!!

Muhammad (*shouting as Vernon screams*) Allah! Sa'idoony! [Help!]

Vernon Jesus Christ!

Pause

Muhammad OK. I make telephone taxi, ana asaweeha. [I'll do it myself.] (*He puts the telephone on the table, and sits. He picks up the receiver. He flicks and pats the telephone, helplessly*)

Jackie gets up and goes over to him. He gestures for her to dial

Jackie Excuse me. Did you ask if you could use that?

Muhammad looks questioningly at her. Jackie puts the telephone back on the unit

---

[13] This is an impossible question. I am an Arab. You shouldn't ask an Arab about his wife! You shouldn't ask him about his religion! It is rude! You are rude, you English! I am an Arab, OK?

You don't just pick up people's phones without asking, you know? Costs money.

Frankie Well, he's got plenty of that, hasn't he?

Jackie That's not the point. (*She sits down again*)

Pause

Vernon No. I'd like to see him telephone for a taxi. Come on! Telephone for a taxi! Is good. OK. Telephone taxi! (*He puts the telephone in front of Muhammad*)

Irving Help yourself!

Jackie gets up and goes to the bar

Vernon Very good, OK, telephone taxi!

Irving There you go—that's it.

Muhammad OK?

Vernon OK!

Pause. Then Muhammad picks up the receiver, and puts it to his ear

Muhammad Taxi?

Vernon and Irving laugh uproariously. Irving's mirth subsides reasonably soon, and he goes over to the bar, where Jackie is pouring herself a drink. But Vernon's laugh is long and loud and rude

Irving (*to Jackie*) You all right?

Jackie Yeh. Just 'aving a whisky.

Vernon How are you, Frankie? All right?

Frankie Yes, thank you.

Vernon Hey, d'you know what? If you weren't a married woman, I could fancy you. How are you, Jackie—all right?

Jackie Yeh I'm all right; are you all right? (*She sits on the sofa*)

Vernon So-so.

Irving (*to Frankie*) You all right?

Frankie Sod off!

Jackie Charming.

Vernon laughs

Frankie (*to Jackie*) What are you staring at?

Jackie stares Frankie out

Jackie How long you been working at your place?

Irving Five years.

Jackie Oh, really, yeh, d'you like it?

Irving Oh, yeh.

Jackie What's the management like?

Irving (*sitting next to her*) Harold? Oh, well he's retiring at the end of the year.

Jackie Oh, really?

Irving Yeh, not before time, either. (*He lights a cigarette*)

Jackie Yeh?—'e's a bit past it, yeh?

Irving He's still living in the nineteen thirties, you know. Thinks it's all done by gentlemen's agreement.

Jackie Yeh; you can't do that, can you?

Irving He wants to move over—give a younger man a chance.

Vernon You ought to apply for that, Irving. Put it in writing. Step up the ladder for you.

Irving Yeh, I might just do that. (*He flicks ash into the ashtray across Jackie*)

Frankie Oh yeh—that'll be the day.

Jackie You wanna grab the opportunity—you know?

Irving You wanna grab everything while you can, don't you? (*He laughs uproariously, briefly*)

Jackie D'you want the ashtray, yeh?

Irving I can reach.

Jackie You have it—it's going on my skirt. (*She passes the ashtray to him*)

Irving Oh, right.

Jackie Well, if a bloke can't do 'is job, you've got to get rid of 'im, you know, you can't afford to carry passengers.

Irving He ought to retire early, really—give other people the opportunity, I mean, there's so much unemployment about today—

Jackie They don't look for jobs, half of them, do they?

Irving No—nation of layabouts we're breeding, aren't we?

Muhammad is drinking the melon "juice" with a spoon

Vernon Is good, yes, you like. Very, very good, OK, shookra, very good, very good, me Tarzan, you Jane!

Irving Here, Sambo: when you've finished that, we've got a nice piece of steak for you!!

Vernon and Irving laugh uproariously

Frankie Oh, leave off, for Christ's sake! (*She goes and sits with Muhammad*) Now then . . . I want you to tell me all about your life in the desert.

Jackie Mind my skirt, yeh?

Irving I'll mind your skirt . . .

Jackie (*getting up*) You want to tell him to watch what 'e's doing with 'is 'ands, Ver.

Jackie exits to the toilet

Vernon You been misbehaving, Irving?

Irving What?

Frankie He's disgusting.

Irving Eh?

Pause

Vernon (*to Muhammad*) You want a drink, Sooty?

Frankie Would you like another orange juice?

Irving I'll get him an orange juice.

Vernon Thank you, Irving.

Irving goes to the bar, and pours Muhammad's drink. Unseen by the others, he adds brandy and gin to the orange juice as well as whisky. Pause

Vernon All right, are you? Happy now? Got yourself a little friend to talk to now, have you? That's nice!

Irving There we are. Drop of whisky.

Frankie I'll take it.

Irving Hang on, dash of soda.

Frankie takes the drink to Muhammad. The toilet flushes, off

There you are, Sambo—that'll make your hair curl.

Vernon What d'you give him, Irving?

Irving Orange juice.

Frankie Here you are. Drink it up.

Irving goes out to the hall, and meets Jackie on her way back from the toilet

Jackie What's the matter?

Irving Nothing.

Jackie Just goin' to powder me nose.

Jackie exits to her room, followed by Irving

Vernon pulls Frankie into a passionate embrace

Irving (*off*) This your room, is it?

Jackie (*off*) Yeh, can you do us a favour, and leave us?

Irving (*off*) Nice, isn't it?

Jackie (*off*) Yes, it is. All right?

Jackie slams the door, off

Irving comes back into the room

Vernon releases Frankie just in time

Vernon Watch your step, Irving—right?

Irving I'm all right. You all right, Sambo, are you, eh? (*He laughs uproariously*)

Frankie adjusts her make-up

Jackie enters

Jackie (*under her breath*) Cigarette . . .

She gets one out. Irving lights it for her

Thank you. (*She sits in the armchair*)

Vernon goes to the music centre. Irving hovers round Jackie. Pause

Irving Got nice legs, haven't you?

Vernon Jesus Christ!

Frankie Irving!
Irving Well, she has, hasn't she? Eh?
Jackie What're you putting on, Vern?
Vernon What d'you fancy, Jackie?
Jackie (*joining Vernon*) Oh, I dunno. Put some Barry Manilow on.
Frankie Rod Stewart?
Vernon Barry Manilow.
Jackie Yeh—I like 'im.
Irving He's a bit immature, though, isn't he?
Jackie Yeh, 'e's nice-looking, though.

Vernon puts on the record. The music starts

Yeh, it's nice.

*Vernon and Frankie gravitate to the bar, and vaguely bop. Jackie returns to
the armchair, and sits in it. Irving continues to hover around her. Muhammad
stands up*

Irving Look, about this test drive ... we've got a blue MGB in the
showroom—
Jackie No, I don't really want one at the moment.
Irving I could bring it round any time—we're only round the corner.
Jackie I 'aven't really got time, you know, I'm very busy in my line.
Irving Well, just give it a try—you're not under any obligation.
Jackie Yeh, I know that—it's no use trying to sell to me, you know—I'm
an old hand at that game.
Irving What about Thursday?
Jackie Would you get me another whisky, yeh?
Irving Soda? Same again?
Jackie Yeh. Fifty-fifty.

*Irving goes to the bar. Muhammad has been standing up for some time, and
is now very drunk. He now lurches towards Jackie. She gets up. The others
do not take any notice of this, or what follows*

What's the matter? Come and sit down, yeh? Don't pull the furniture
around! What're you doing?

*Muhammad turns Jackie upside down, picks her up bodily, and bears her out
of the room*

(*Calling*) Vernon !! Vernon!!

Vernon and Irving run to her rescue in the hall

Vernon Jesus Bloody Christ!
Irving Here—put her down.
Jackie Vern—get him off me!
Irving Get hold of her, right?
Frankie Jesus Christ!
Irving You filthy Arab, you get off her!

Irving pulls Muhammad off Jackie, thrusting him so hard that he staggers backwards into Frankie's arms in the room

Jackie (*to Irving*) Get off me.
Irving (*to Jackie*) All right, all right, all right.

Vernon goes to Frankie and Muhammad, who is hardly conscious

(*Groping*) You want a hand up?

Jackie Look, sod off, will you? Vern!
Irving Don't you want a hand up?
Jackie Sod off! Vern!!

Vernon What's going on? What're you playing at? What's your game, eh?

Vernon goes to Jackie's rescue. Frankie is propping up the virtually unconscious Muhammad

Vernon Irying! What're you up to?
Irving Just trying to pick her up.
Vernon Get off her. You were having a bloody grope, weren't you?
Irving You're not going to leave her on the floor, are you?
Vernon You've had your hands on her all night!

Frankie It's all right . . . I've got you, don't worry . . . I've got you . . . Jesus Christ! What a weight.

Irving goes into the room

Are you all right, Jackie?
Jackie Just get 'im out of 'ere, Vern!

Irving violently pulls Muhammad away from Frankie

Irving You get off her!!
Frankie Irving!!
Vernon Mind that bar!

Irving frog-marches Muhammad round the sofa

Irving I'll have you, you Arab, you bastard!!
Vernon Watch out, Irving—mind the glasses!!

Irving throws Muhammad headlong on to the sofa, causing an ashtray to be thrown on to the floor scattering its contents

Frankie ⎱ (*together*) ⎰ Look what you've done, you stupid bugger!
Vernon ⎰   ⎱ You slob, Irving!

Vernon exits to the kitchen

Irving You keep your filthy hands off my wife! (*To Frankie*) What were you doing, eh?
Frankie Eh?
Irving I saw you!
Frankie I wasn't doing anything!
Irving Rubbing your body up against him!

Frankie Don't be so disgusting, Irving, for Christ's sake!

Jackie comes into the room and sets about trying to find her cigarettes

Jackie (*under her breath*) Cigarettes . . .

Vernon enters with the dustpan and brush

Muhammad surfaces slightly and tries to get hold of Jackie

Muhammad Jack . . .

Jackie Just get off me, yeh?

Irving hears this, and proceeds to assault Muhammad

Vernon (*to Muhammad*) Hey! You! Get off her!

Irving (*attempting to assault Muhammad*) Get back! You get back!

Vernon (*intercepting*) Irving!!

Irving I'll get you!! I'll do for you!!

Vernon Get off, Irving! Keep out of it, for Christ's sake!!

Muhammad staggers behind the sofa

Jackie Ver! Ver, get him out of 'ere, I don't wannim 'ere!

Vernon You brought him here, Jackie.

Jackie I didn't! I didn't!

Vernon He's your friend, Jackie—

Jackie I don't wannim 'ere—I didn't!

Vernon He's your responsibility, right—you brought him here. (*He turns off the music centre and resumes cleaning up*)

Frankie Leave off, for Christ's sake —Irving, leave him alone!!

Irving What's the matter with you, eh? You a wog-lover now, are you?

Frankie For Christ's sake, Irving— don't be so bloody stupid! You gone bloody mad, or something?

Irving You slut!! You cow!!

Frankie Jesus Christ, Irving, stop it, for God's sake!!

Irving (*shouting*) Why don't you just suck him off, eh?

Frankie (*shouting*) Oh, for Christ's sake, Irving, don't be so disgusting!!

Irving (*shouting*) Go on—get inside his trousers! We all know what you're after—why don't you just get on with it?

Muhammad appears from behind the sofa and vomits on to it

Vernon (*shouting*) Oh my God! You disgusting animal!!!!

Frankie Oo-ugh!

Vernon exits to the kitchen, fast

Irving You've got a damned cheek! You did that on purpose, didn't you?

Vernon enters, fast, with a plastic washing-up bowl

Irving and Vernon put Muhammad's head in the bowl, and force him into a kneeling position on the floor with it

Vernon In there. In there. Good, in there, see, there, right?

During the following passage, Muhammad continues to vomit intermittently, but audibly

Irving What a waste of booze!

Vernon What d'you give him, Irving?

Irving Orange juice.

Vernon What d'you put in it?

Irving Whisky.

Vernon What else?

Irving You've been giving him whisky all night.

Vernon He can take whisky, can't he?—that's his drink—he brought that bottle.

Irving No, they're not used to it—they can't hold it!

Vernon What else, Irving?

Irving Nothing!

Frankie Irving!

Irving You shut up!!

Vernon What else, for Christ's sake?

Irving Brandy and gin.

Vernon ⎫ *(together)* ⎧ You ignorant twit——
Frankie ⎭   ⎩ Jesus Christ, you stupid bugger!

Vernon —you fucking moron—you're worse than him!

Vernon exits to the kitchen

Frankie You bastard—what d'you think you're playing at? Eh?

Irving He would have thrown up, anyway.

Frankie Don't be so bloody stupid!!

Vernon enters

Jackie Ver—can I have a whisky?

Frankie goes to the phone and begins to dial

Irving You put that down!

Frankie Jesus Christ, Irving!

Irving You touch that phone, I'll ring your neck!!

Frankie (*backing away round the room*) Don't you threaten me!!

Irving I'll do more than threaten you!

Jackie Please, Ver. Ver!

Vernon What, Jackie?

Jackie Can I 'ave a whisky?

Vernon He just poured you a whisky, didn't he?

Jackie I want you to pour me one.

Vernon If you don't want that whisky, help yourself to another one from the bar, for Christ's sake!!

Jackie Please, Ver!

Frankie You stay where you are! Don't you come near me!

Irving I wouldn't soil my hands!

Frankie For Christ's sake, Irving! You've gone bloody daft—you've got a bloody screw loose!

Irving Why don't you sit down, eh? Take the weight off your feet?

Muhammad makes another vague attempt to get hold of Jackie from his position on the floor

Muhammad Make taxi!
Jackie Get off me!
Irving (*going for Muhammad*) You leave her alone!!
Vernon Irving!
Irving All right, all right, Vernon—just watch him, eh?
Vernon Keep out of it—mind you own business.
Irving Look—it is my business: he's been mauling my wife!
Vernon Oh, shut up!
Muhammad Make taxi! Make taxi!
Vernon Oh, Christ! He's going to be sick again. In there. In there, see. There, there, there, there. Right?

Frankie and Jackie edge out of the room

Muhammad Make taxi! Make taxi! Make taxi! (*He starts to cry, but is not sick. Throughout the following speeches, he continues to cry and whimper "Make taxi!"*)

Frankie creeps back into the room

Irving Oh for God's sake! Why don't you grow up? You cry-baby! What's the matter? You homesick, or something?
Frankie Jesus Christ, Irving!
Irving Here, Vernon, you got any sand? Sprinkle it round his feet, make him feel at home!
Muhammad Make taxi . . . Allah, allah . . .
Vernon Irving, you really are a berk, aren't you?

Vernon exits to the kitchen

Frankie goes to Muhammad

Frankie Oh, Christ! I can't bear seeing a man cry!
Irving You keep away from him!
Frankie (*shouting*) You shut up!
Irving (*seizing her*) Don't you touch him!
Frankie Leave me alone, Irving, for Christ's sake!
Irving You keep right away from him, right?!
Frankie For Christ's sake, Irving, leave me!
Irving Just keep away!
Frankie Just leave me alone!
Irving You slut!
Frankie Oh, Jesus Christ!
Irving (*shouting*) I'll kill you!!

Vernon enters

Frankie } (*together; shouting*) { Vernon!!
Irving }   { I'll kill you!!

Frankie ⎫
Muhammad ⎬ *(together)* ⎰ Vernon!! Vernon!!
Vernon ⎭   ⎰ *(shouting)* Taxi! Taxi! Taxi!
                              (almost inaudibly) You all right, Jackie? I'll get
                              rid of them.

Irving Oh yeh? Vernon? Vernon? Shout for Vernon! We all know about Vernon.

Vernon What do you know about Vernon?

Irving I know about you two. I know you've been having it off.

Vernon You what?!

Irving You've been having it off, haven't you?

Vernon You must be bloody joking. Right. The party's over. Piss off!

Pause

Irving Haven't you been having it off, then?

Vernon Irving: I wouldn't stoop so low.

Frankie *Oh!!*

Vernon Come on. Chop-chop. Closing time. Get out, and take your fat wife with you.

Frankie Oh!

Irving Right: time to go home, is it?

Vernon Time to go home.

Irving OK. (*He throws Frankie's bag into her lap*) Get your coat.

Frankie You get my bloody coat!

Irving *You get your coat!*

He throws her on to the floor

   She gets up, and goes out for her coat

Irving Right. Thanks, Vernon. It's been a nice evening. I'll see you Monday, right?

Vernon See you Monday, Irving.

Irving Give my love to Astrid.

   Frankie enters with her coat

Frankie Come on, for Christ's sake!

Irving Where are you going?

Frankie To get my cigarettes.

Frankie goes to the bar, where Vernon is; Irving goes into the dining area, where Jackie is

Irving I'll phone you in the week, Jackie, all right? (*He pinches her bottom*)

Jackie (*under her breath*) Get off!!

   Irving laughs uproariously, then exits

Frankie (*quietly*) Are you going to phone me, Vern?

Vernon (*quietly*) Call you Monday, Frankie.

Frankie (*quietly*) Right.

Irving (*off*) Come on!
Frankie (*going towards the hall*) I'm coming.

Frankie exits. Vernon follows her

Irving (*off*) Have you got the keys?
Frankie (*off*) Course I've got the bloody keys!
Irving (*off*) Well, I'm driving—right?
Frankie (*off*) No, you're not!

The front door opens, off

Irving (*off*) Look, I'm doing the driving!
Frankie (*off*) It's my car, Irving!
Vernon (*off*) 'Bye, now! Safe journey!

The front door slams, off

Vernon enters

(*Muttering*) Jesus Christ!

Muhammad attempts to light a cigarette. Vernon takes the cigarette out of of his mouth, and confiscates the matches

Oh, no, you don't—not in your state, you'll set the bloody place on fire. (*He picks up the bowl*) Keep an eye on him, Jackie.

Vernon exits to the toilet

Pause

Muhammad La. La. La. La. Mā dām Muhammad ygooloon "La"' Amma Ibraheem aw Marwan 'ala kaifhum! Lākin Muhammad "La"! La. La. L'abbid. Roohu intum yam; Ibraheem aw Marwan ila London. Twannisu! Ishrabu! Dakhinu! Lākin Muhammad? La! Muhammad? Hadha kelb! Hadha h'marr! Hadha akmak! Ammar Bandar aw Turki aw Ahmad aw Selmaan aw Alawi aw Hisham 'ala kaifhum! Roohu intum ila Beirut aw Qaahirah. Twannisu . . .[14]

Jackie bolts over to the bar

Jack? . . . Is Frank? . . . Is Jack? OK, I speak . . . OK? OK. OK, you speak wife. Is . . . I go Taif . . . is camel make . . . (*He makes an arm-ripping gesture*) I go Abha, is make . . . (*He pauses*) Allah. Allah. Allah. Is—is—is (*He pounds himself*) Ya ba'ad galby.[15] (*He punches the*

---

[14] No. No. No. No. If it's Muhammad the answer is "No". As for Ibraheem and Marwan they can do as they like! But Muhammad "No"! No. No. Absolutely not. Everybody else go; Ibraheem and Marwan to London. Have a good time! Drink! Smoke! But Muhammad? No! Muhammad? He is a dog! He is a donkey! He is an idiot! As for Bandar and Turki and Hisham they can do whatever they like! Everybody go to Beirut and Cairo. Have a good time . . .

[15] Oh, one after my heart. (You are my ideal girl.)

sofa once) No . . . eh . . . speak . . . ya ba'ad galby! (*He punches the sofa twice*)

Jackie Don't bang that settee!

Muhammad raises himself up, and makes a final tortuous attempt to communicate with Jackie: it is identifiable with clarity neither in English nor in Arabic. It builds to a painful climax, and then Muhammad collapses on the floor

What's the matter with you? Get up on the settee? Get up, yeh? 'S the matter with you?

She tries to lift him on to the sofa, and fails, winding up on the floor with him, exhausted and fraught

Vernon enters

Vernon What's going on, Jackie?

Jackie Just trying to get him on the settee.

Pause. Jackie kneels up. Vernon stands by her. He touches her hair

I don't even know him. I know 'is friend, you know—he's really nice.

Vernon You've got to be careful with these geezers. Can't trust them, can you?

Jackie I don't want him here!!

Vernon You brought him here, Jackie. (*He moves away to the bar. He takes a swig of his drink*) Right. Let's get this monkey on his feet. (*He goes to Muhammad*) Come on. On your feet. Come on, get up. Get up. Wake up. (*He smacks Muhammad's face*) Come on. Time to go home! On your feet! Come on! Get up! For Christ's sake. Come on! Christ; he's spark out, isn't he?

Jackie Mm. That settee all right, Ver?

Vernon Suppose so.

Jackie If there's any sick-stains or anything on the carpet, Abdullah'll pay for it. Come out of 'is expenses.

Vernon He'll pay for it himself.

Jackie Yeh, he's got the money.

Vernon Where's he keep it?

Jackie In his trousers.

Vernon takes out the wad of money, and inspects it

You wanna keep some of that, and pay for the damages.

Vernon There's nothing damaged, is there? (*He puts the money back*) It'll pay for his bloody taxi, anyway, won't it?

Jackie What you gonna do?

Vernon Leave him.

Jackie If you stick him in a taxi, they can shove him off at the hotel.

Vernon I can't stick him in a taxi—look at the size of him. I can't shift him down two flights of stairs.

Jackie You can't just leave 'im there.

Vernon Yeh: let him sleep it off. Do him good.

Pause

Jackie Ver ...
Vernon What?
Jackie Can I have a whisky?
Vernon What d'you want? Mine or his?
Jackie I don't want 'is!

Vernon pours the whisky. He picks up the water jug

Can I have soda?

He gives her soda. He puts her drink on the bar

Vernon There you are. (*He proceeds to empty ashtrays into the dustpan*)
Cost me a bloody fortune tonight. Those Gammons. They're gannets!
Jackie That bloke think you was up to something?
Vernon What?
Jackie With 'is wife?
Vernon Who? Irving?
Jackie Yeh.
Vernon Yes, he did, didn't he?
Jackie Yeh.
Vernon No way—d'you see her?
Jackie Yeh, I did.
Vernon Yuk!

> *Vernon exits to the kitchen to put the dustpan away. He turns out the
> kitchen light and returns*

Jackie See what 'e did to me when 'e went?
Vernon No, what d'e do?
Jackie Put 'is 'and up my skirt.
Vernon Did he? Jesus Christ, there's something the matter with that guy,
I tell you.

Vernon switches off the lamp on the bar, then the lamp on the wall-unit

Right. I've had enough. I'm turning in. Get some shuteye. (*He stands
near Jackie*) Look at him. Quite sweet, isn't he?

*Vernon draws Jackie to him. She is resistant at first, but only for a few
moments. He kisses her rapaciously, and for quite a long time. When the kiss
is over, she gasps. He still holds her in an embrace. She whimpers into his
chest*

Why don't you stay with me tonight? That's your best bet. Then if he
wakes up, you'll be all right.
Jackie I dunno ...

He releases her. He goes to the door

Vernon Think about it.

Vernon switches off the main light and exits to his room

Pause. Jackie goes to get one of her cigarettes. She lights one. Muhammad starts to move. Pause. Muhammad starts to snore. Jackie goes into the hall, closing the door behind her. She closes the other door

    Jackie exits

The hall light goes out, and Vernon's door closes, off. Silence. Muhammad snores. The Lights slowly fade to a—

BLACK-OUT

FURNITURE AND PROPERTY LIST

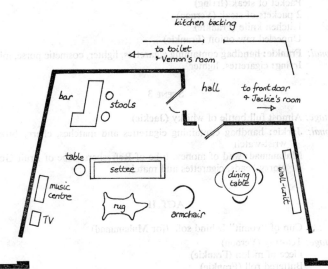

ACT I

SCENE 1

On stage: Black leather sofa

Black leather swivel armchair

Side table. *On it:* ashtray, table lighter

Music centre. *Under it:* cassettes and records

Bar. *On it:* ashtrays, ice bucket, water-jug, soda syphon, table lamp (practical). *Behind bar:* various bottles of drink including gin, whisky, vodka, brandy, tonic water, orange juice, tea-towel, glasses

Bar-stools. *On one:* executive case containing diary, pocket calculator.

Television

Dining-table. *On it:* squash racket

4 dining-chairs

Wall unit. *On shelves:* small nude female statuette, car brochure, a few paperbacks, 2 or 3 small school sports trophies, telephone, table lamp (practical). *In cupboards underneath:* table mats, napkins, cutlery, crockery, cruet set, wine glasses

On walls: several mirrors, veteran car motifs

Imitation leopard-skin rug

Carpet

SCENE 2

Off stage: Tray of nuts **(Vernon)**
  Butter, basket with bread rolls, 3 plates of melon **(Vernon)**
  Wrapped bottle of red wine **(Irving)**
  Opened bottle of white wine **(Vernon)**
  2 plates of melon **(Vernon)**
  Naughty apron **(Vernon)**
  Packet of steak **(Irving)**
  2 packets of steak **(Vernon)**
  Kitchen knife **(Frankie)**
  Unpeeled raw onion **(Frankie)**

Personal: **Frankie:** handbag containing cigarettes, lighter, cosmetic purse, mirror
  Irving: cigarettes, lighter

SCENE 3

Off stage: Almost full bottle of whisky **(Jackie)**

Personal: **Jackie:** handbag containing cigarettes and matches, cherry brooch,
    wrist-watch
  Muhammad: wad of money, tube of Refreshers, tube of Fruit Gums,
    worry beads, cigarettes and matches

ACT II

Set: Cup of "vomit" behind sofa (for **Muhammad**)
Off stage: Tea-tray **(Vernon)**
  Piece of melon **(Frankie)**
  Buttered roll **(Frankie)**
  Dustpan **(Vernon)**
  Dish of melon and spoon **(Frankie)**
  Sugar-bowl **(Jackie)**
  Dustpan and brush **(Vernon)**
  Washing-up bowl **(Vernon)**

LIGHTING PLOT

Practical fittings required: 2 table lamps, pendant in main room, light in hall,
    light in kitchen
Interior. A flat. The same scene throughout

ACT I, Scene 1   Early morning

To open: General effect of early morning light

Cue 1   **Jackie** exits to her room   (Page 4)
          Quick fade to Black-out

ACT I, Scene 2   Early evening

To open: All interior lighting on

Cue 2   **Vernon** switches off lamp on bar   (Page 17)
          Snap off lamp on bar and covering spots

Cue 3   **Vernon** switches off lamp on wall-unit   (Page 17)
          Snap off lamp on wall-unit and covering spots

Cue 4   **Vernon** switches off main light   (Page 17)
          Snap off pendant

Cue 5   **Vernon** switches off kitchen light   (Page 17)
          Snap off kitchen light

Cue 6   **Vernon** (*off*): "I know the way, Irving."   (Page 18)
          Snap off hall light

Cue 7   **Vernon** (*off*): "I'll do it my way, Irving."   (Page 18)
          Pause, then fairly quick fade to Black-out

ACT I, Scene 3   Evening

To open: Darkness

Cue 8   **Jackie** (*off*): "Just go through."   (Page 18)
          Snap on hall light

Cue 9   **Jackie** switches on main light   (Page 18)
          Snap on pendant

Cue 10 **Jackie** switches on lamp on wall-unit   (Page 18)
          Snap on lamp on wall-unit and covering spots

Cue 11 **Jackie** switches on lamp on bar   (Page 19)
          Snap on lamp on bar and covering spots

Cue 12 **Muhammad** switches off main light   (Page 29)
          Snap off pendant

Cue 13 **Jackie** switches on main light   (Page 29)
          Snap on pendant

Cue 14	**Muhammad** switches off main light	(Page 29)
	Snap off pendant	
Cue 15	**Jackie** switches on main light	(Page 29)
	Snap on pendant	
Cue 16	**Muhammad** switches off lamp on bar	(Page 29)
	Snap off lamp on bar and covering spots	
Cue 17	**Jackie** switches on lamp on bar	(Page 29)
	Snap on lamp on bar and covering spots	
Cue 18	**Vernon:** "*A bloody Arab!!*"	(Page 32)
	Black-out	

ACT II Evening

To open: All interior lighting on

Cue 19	**Vernon** switches off kitchen light	(Page 77)
	Snap off kitchen light	
Cue 20	**Vernon** switches off lamp on bar	(Page 77)
	Snap off lamp on bar and covering spots	
Cue 21	**Vernon** switches off lamp on wall-unit	(Page 77)
	Snap off lamp on wall-unit and covering spots	
Cue 22	**Vernon** switches off main light	(Page 77)
	Snap off pendant	
Cue 23	**Jackie** exits	(Page 78)
	Snap off hall light	
Cue 24	**Muhammad** snores	(Page 78)
	Slow fade to Black-out	

EFFECTS PLOT

ACT I

Cue 19	**Irving**: ". . . dash of soda." *Toilet flushes, off*	(Page 68)
Cue 20	**Jackie** (*off*): "Yes, it is. All right?" *Door slams off* L	(Page 68)
Cue 21	**Vernon** starts music centre *Pause, then bring up music: Barry Manilow*	(Page 69)
Cue 22	**Vernon** turns off music centre *Snap off music*	(Page 71)
Cue 23	**Frankie** (*off*): "No, you're not!" *Front door opens, off* L	(Page 75)
Cue 24	**Vernon** (*off*): "Safe journey!" *Front door slams, off* L	(Page 75)
Cue 25	Hall light goes out *Door closes, off* R	(Page 78)

MADE AND PRINTED IN GREAT BRITAIN BY
LATIMER TREND & COMPANY LTD PLYMOUTH
MADE IN ENGLAND